IF
GOD
WANTED US
TO TRAVEL . . .

ALSO BY THE AUTHOR

Soft Pretzels with Mustard
Revenge Is the Best Exercise
Nobody Ever Sees You Eat Tuna Fish

IF
GOD
WANTED US
TO TRAVEL . . .

DAVID BRENNER

POCKET BOOKS

New York   London   Toronto   Sydney   Tokyo   Singapore

An *Original* Publication of POCKET BOOKS

POCKET BOOKS, a division of Simon & Schuster Inc.
1230 Avenue of the Americas, New York, NY 10020

Brenner, David, 1945–
    If God wanted us to travel / David Brenner.
        p.   cm.
    ISBN 0-671-70113-4 : $16.95
    1. Travel—Humor. 2. Business travel—Humor. I. Title.
PN6231.T7B7   1990
818'.5402—dc20   90-6897
                                                                       CIP

First Pocket Books printing June 1990

10   9   8   7   6   5   4   3   2   1

Design by Stanley S. Drate/Folio Graphics Co. Inc.

Printed in the U.S.A.

TO

my mother and father, who taught
me how to look for and find the
beauty and humor in life, and to my
eight-year-old son, Cole Jay,
to whom this wondrous world will
soon belong.

ACKNOWLEDGMENTS

In alphabetical order, I thank the following persons for their invaluable help in writing this book:

Ronnie Berger, my travel agent, for all the years of getting me through the horrors of travel with as few scratches and nervous breakdowns as possible.

My sister, Bib, and my brother, Moby, for making so many trips so much more enjoyable.

Childhood friends—"Beb" and Lenore Black, "Dee Dee" Romoff, Morty "The Bird" and Marcia Hoffman, Stan "The Dancer" Levinson, and "Moose" and Rita Caruso—for sharing in so many good times away from the old neighborhood.

Robert Cinque, my attorney, for keeping the lawsuits to a minimum, so I'd have the time to write this book.

My fans, who have made all the wonderful things possible.

Stuart Krichevsky, my literary agent, for believing in the idea and then selling it.

Artie Moskowitz, my agent, who got me enough work through the years enabling me to travel.

Susan Murphy, my secretary, for not complaining about all the photocopying and for taking care of my life.

Dr. Milton Reder for keeping my bad back in good enough condition to travel and then to sit for hours writing about it.

Steve Reidman, my manager, who, were this not in alphabetical order, would be first on the list as the most helpful in writing the book and for all he has done for my career.

George Schultz for all the hysterical laughter he generated on so many trips.

Dave Shalek for all the strong cappuccinos.

Nick Siracuse for all his creative contributions.

Elizabeth Slater for her support, comments, and shared moments traveling.

Leslie Wells, my editor, without whose help this book would be 5,000 pages long, and for buying the idea as soon as she heard it.

Steve Wynn for allowing me to pound the typewriter all night long, night after night, at his Golden Nugget Hotel.

Bill Zysblat, my business manager, for clearing my head of all financial matters so I could be creative.

CONTENTS

Travel Quotes   xiii
Prologue   xvii

◆ ◆ ◆ **WHERE TO GO?** ◆ ◆ ◆

Where to Go? / 3
The Great Outdoors / 4
What's Your Sign? / 8
Who Buys It? / 9
Things You Hate to Hear / 11
Native Dress / 12
If We Skip Lunch / 13
The Little Darlings / 15
Not on Any Map / 17
What's Your Sign? / 18
Go or No Go? / 19

◆ ◆ ◆ **PREPARING FOR** ◆ ◆ ◆
YOUR TRIP

You Can't Miss It / 25
What's Your Sign? / 31

Things You'll Never See When You Are Traveling / 33
A Pack Rat / 34
Don't Fly It; Fly It / 35
People Lie, Not Numbers / 36
What's Your Sign? / 41
Enough Is More Than Enough / 43
Child Prevention / 43
Too Long, Too Often / 45
Only the Scenery / 46
Home Secure Home / 48
Things You'll Never Hear / 51

◆ ◆ ◆ **HELPFUL FACTS** ◆ ◆ ◆
& TIPS

Two Fat, Bald Women / 55
Tales of the Very Old Wives / 56
Adoo, Bar, and Reem / 61
What's Your Sign? / 63
Travel Babble / 64
Common Sen-Sen Sense / 73
Things You Hate to See / 74
So, What's It Like? / 75
What's Your Sign? / 75
Help! / 77
Love It or Leave It / 84
The Car, James / 86
Help Is Only a Fingertip Away / 87
The World's Lightest Luggage / 90
More Things You'll Never Hear / 92

◆ ◆ ◆ **GETTING THERE** ◆ ◆ ◆

A Flying Vacillation / 97
What's Your Sign? / 98
Tick Tock, Tick Tock / 100
You Name It, I Got It / 101
More Things You Hate to See / 105
Up, Up, and Not Away / 106
Foreign Foolery / 107
Don't Look, Don't Talk / 107
The Lord Has Landed / 109
A Different Perspective / 109
Say What? / 111
Size 10D / 118
Drive Carefully / 120
Dying for Profit / 121
Never Too Safe / 122

◆ ◆ ◆ **HOTELS &** ◆ ◆ ◆
RESTAURANTS

More Things You Hate to See / 125
Gulliver Slept Here / 126
Checkout Time / 127
What's Your Sign? / 130
Thank You, Mr. President / 132
No Clinks, No Clanks / 136
The Commodian / 136
Three on a Match / 138
Money Talks in the Morning / 139
H.H. Himself / 140
My Favorite Flying Joke / 144
Water, Water Everywhere / 144

◆ ◆ ◆ **SIGHT-SEEING** ◆ ◆ ◆

Wish You Were Here / 149
The Old Man and the Road / 150
Signs of Our Times / 152
More Things You Hate to Hear / 154
Threatened in Spain / 156
What's Your Sign? / 158
You'd Better Not / 160
What's Your Sign? / 171
Wax Johnson / 172
Honoring the Competition / 178
More Things You Hate to Hear / 181
Pleeze, Mistah / 182
Lower the Drawbridge / 183
Four One-Dollar Bills / 185
You'd Better Not / 187

◆ ◆ ◆ **RETURNING
HOME** ◆ ◆ ◆

Hi, Operator / 195
What's Your Sign? / 196
Who, What, Where, When, & Why? / 198
Your Duty-Free Duty / 202
Too Long, Too Often / 203
Unaccustomed Customs / 208
If God Wanted Us to Travel . . . / 210

Epilogue   215

❝It's a magnificent ship. What powers it?❞

—Anonymous Slave
Seeing Long-Oared Warship
Delos
227 B.C.

❝I think it's that way.❞

—Christopher Columbus
Madrid, Spain
February 17, 1492

❝Bitburg? I thought they said Pittsburgh.❞

—Ronald Reagan
Visiting Nazi SS Graveyard
Bitburg, Germany
May 5, 1985

❝Vere you goin'? Sit. Vat's your hurry?❞

—Every Retired Jewish Man
Miami Beach, Florida
1921–Today

IF
GOD
WANTED US
TO TRAVEL ...

PROLOGUE

I love travel. More than almost anyone. I got the bug from my parents, who took off whenever they could, even though they were always poor and living on the very edge of a tight budget all their lives. Usually, they drove in their old car to towns and cities along the Eastern seaboard, close to our hometown of Philadelphia. I saved extra money working overtime when I was fourteen years old and sent them on a two-week vacation to Canada, their first time out of the country. As family fortunes improved, I was able to send them on several three-month cruises around the entire world. I've seen the better part of the world myself. As a matter of fact, if we were to include my brother, sister, and the rest of the Brenner clan, I think that collectively there is hardly a country in the world that has not been visited by one or more of us.

Yes, I love travel, but I hate traveling! Ideally, I want to close my eyes, think of the place to which I'm going, and POP! I'm there. Another POP! and my rental car is in the parking lot and I am in my hotel room. I despise every means of transportation and every hassle involved in getting from my home to where I'm going and back again. From the moment I first think of taking a trip, I begin to panic. My attitude and motto is "A vacation doesn't begin until the last hanger is hung up in the closet." In other words, only when I have unpacked the last item in my bag and have placed it in the closet, in the room I am supposed to get, in the hotel I am supposed to be in, do I relax and begin my vacation.

There are so many things that can go wrong. Over the years I have compiled a total of 1,248 things that can go awry from the time you are preparing to leave your home until you are settled at your destination. Just to give you a very limited scenario of what I worry about when beginning a vacation:

The alarm doesn't go off. It goes off, but it is set for the wrong time. It is set for the right time, but the clock was not turned forward for daylight saving time. You remembered to push the clock ahead, but you can't find a taxi to take you to the airport. You get a cab, but the driver doesn't know the way to the airport. He knows the way, but is caught in traffic. He isn't caught in traffic and gets to the airport in time, but it is the wrong airport. It's the right one, but your flight is canceled. Your flight is not canceled, but is several hours late. It takes off on time, but has to return for an emergency landing. It doesn't have to return, but it crashes. It doesn't crash, but is forced to land in another city. It lands in the right city, but is boarded by terrorists. There are no terrorists and you deplane, but none of your bags do. Only half of them make it. All of them make it, but they are empty. They are not empty, but they are ripped open. They aren't ripped open, but there are no skycaps. There are skycaps, but they can't find you a cab. . . .

So, I'm a nervous wreck and not on vacation until I put the last hanger in the closet, and not a moment before, because, at one time or another, all the aforementioned disasters and the balance adding up to the 1,248 total have happened to me.

This book contains all the information you need to help you hang up that last hanger. Good luck.

DAVID BRENNER

The above was written by the author while he was waiting for a dinghy to row him to an island where he hoped he could catch a flight home, after his plane's windshield was smashed by low-flying geese who had become disoriented in a freak low fog resulting from the eruption of a volcano on a nearby island at the exact moment of the aircraft's takeoff, forcing the plane to make an emergency landing in the sea in which no lives were lost but all baggage was, except for the author's inflatable carry-on bag, which he had purchased after the first time this exact incident had happened to him almost six years previously to the day (number 988 on the author's list of 1,854 things that could go wrong on the way home).

WHERE TO GO?

◆ ◆ ◆ ◆ ◆ ◆ ◆ ◆ ◆ ◆ ◆

◆ ◆ ◆ Where to Go?

One of the biggest travel dilemmas is where to go. What makes it an even more horrendous problem is the person to whom most people turn for an answer—the Travel Agent. Beware of unscrupulous travel agents. New York to California for one hundred dollars' coach fare may sound great, until you find out that every forty miles, they have to stop the coach to rest the horses.

I'm fortunate because my travel agent, Ronnie, is the best and has taken perfect care of me, my manager, family, and friends for years. I say this out of love and fear, because I don't want to pack for Paris and end up dog-sledding in Alaska.

I am talking about your average travel agent. The one you see through the window in which there are toy models of several ocean liners, a 747 jet, the Concorde, and pictures of exotic lands. The person who looks like the farthest they've traveled is to their refrigerator, telephone, and TV.

I don't know about you, but I have a tough time on a freezing day in mid-February listening with any degree of believability to a pale, almost transparent human being telling me about the wonders of some romantic island in the South Pacific, when in my heart I know the closest she ever came to it was in a movie theater watching Ezio Pinza and Kathryn Grayson sing in front of a fake sunset. How can you get enthusiastic about a daily trek across the

3

plains of Kenya when it is being described to you by someone whose longest daily trek has been transporting her 240 pounds from her desk to the water cooler?

· Would you go to a dentist who has no teeth or listen to the perfect blackjack system from someone lying in the gutter? When I'm thinking of going somewhere, I want someone who's been there, has done it, seen it, felt it, lived it, not someone who fell asleep during the National Geographic TV series and can't tell the difference between a hippo and a junkyard dog.

So what do you do about where to go? I am confident that if you sat down in your most comfortable chair, put on some quiet music, drink in hand, kicked your shoes off, and allowed your mind to wander freely, you could come up with a list of ten places you'd like to see. Do it. Make the list and then start with number one and work your way around this fabulous world of ours.

▶ ▶ ▶ # The Great Outdoors

I believe one should not reject most aspects of life without first trying them. Well, I have tried The Great Outdoors and I don't like it. I'm speaking specifically about camping, horseback riding, fishing, and hunting. These are the great American pastimes. (The great American putztimes, if you ask me.)

Camping: I can't figure out the joy of carrying a heavy pack anywhere, let alone aboard a bus, train, or plane, and then dragging it all around what is commonly called The Great Outdoors, which is actually the homeland of all kinds of ugly things that crawl, fly, leap, bite, and sting, only to sleep inside a cloth Baggie on the ground, that is, if you are able to close your eyes knowing there is a strong possibility that you will be awakened by the roar of a chain saw in the hands of some demented Neanderthal man who collects human heads for his parents, who are actually brother and sister, and knowing my luck, this defective will find an electrical outlet right outside my tent. No, thank you.

Horseback Riding: I can't figure out why anyone, especially after a tiresome train, plane, bus, or car ride, would want to sit on top of a sweaty, smelly beast of burden who, at best, has an IQ comparable to that of oak tree bark, who will then cause you to sway and bounce up a precarious mountain trail, while you are looking continuously at the asses of the horses in front of you, who often go while on the go, never knowing if the particular animal on which you are sitting may have decided that very morning that it is sick and tired of a life consisting of having strange animals sit on its back seven days a week, fifty-two weeks a year, the reward for which is a bunch of dry hay and a few gulps of bucket water, and the four-legged one has decided he will end it all by leaping off the mountain; but then again, maybe there is a mountain trail or a wide-open plain across which the four-legged mass of stupidity is allowed to run at full speed with enough bounce to his ounce to mix the cement needed to repave the sidewalks in St. Paul and Minneapolis. No, thank you.

Fishing: I can't figure out why anyone would want to arise at five A.M. to drive to a body of water in which he will stand for endless hours, wearing long, rubber diapers, hoping that the stick with the string, on the end of which he has taken a slimy worm and stabbed it through the heart with the hook, will suddenly bend so that he can spend all his energy fighting with a fish whose only sin in life was to be too close to this murderer, and all of this is in hopes that the fish will die, so the hook can then be ripped out of the fish's mouth, a knife can slice open its belly to clean out all the garbage and entrails, so that the man can have the fun of watching it fry, along with the uninvited leaves, twigs, pollen, and insects, after which the fish is eaten. And most important is the joy of telling the story of the big kill to a friend who will try to top it with the story of his own water assassination. No, thank you.

Hunting: I can't figure this one out because it is a combination of the worst of two of the aforementioned, starting with arising with God (see *fishing*) and living outside (see *camping*), and has its own insanity, such as dressing in camouflage clothing, believing that this protects the man from being seen by the animals, which is as ridiculous as a moose walking into your house with a picture of a chair on its side hoping you don't notice him. Then, if the hunter is lucky enough not to be shot by a fellow hunter, he looks through a rifle sight sophisticated enough to enable Stevie Wonder to zero in on a house fly's testicles 400 yards away on a dark night, and presses this metal trigger with the tip of his finger, so far avoiding any need for particular skills or strength, and watching one of Bambi's descendants fall dead to the ground, but instead of being cleaned and fried (see *fishing*), (and this is one of the most fun parts of the activity) it is then tied to the fender of his car and driven to a store where Bambi, Jr., will then have his head chopped off, and (this is definitely the most fun part) is stuffed and given glass eyes and mounted on a wood plaque to be hung up on a wall in his house as proof to all who venture indoors how wonderful he was outdoors, how macho, even though I have suggested at times to these gallant men of deadly fingertips that were they really desirous of testing their machismo then they would hand out little .22-caliber handguns to the rabbits and 30/30 rifles to all the deer and bears in the morning and then return to the woods in the afternoon. But no one wanted to risk being shot, and besides, if they did get shot, it would be cold-blooded murder. No, thank you.

I could add tennis and golf to my list of outdoor activities, but I've probably made enough enemies as it is. However, I would like to say one more thing. I can't figure out why more people don't do what I do outdoors:

Sailing: Ah, the joy of living aboard something that is forty-six feet long and houses seven other human beings who for a week or two will share one, maybe two, bathrooms along with such wonderful experiences as rope burn, windburn, collecting seashells and bruises and cuts, fearing storms that could test how far you can swim, feeling the heat of the sun and sunburn, hearing the rumble of thunder and of your stomach trying to cope with the meat that went bad when the ice melted and no one noticed, looking endlessly at water, lots and lots of water, climbing up a mast to free a tangled line, busting a nail or finger undoing a knot, pulling and tugging lines, feeling the careening boom crash into your forehead on a tack, stubbing your toe on one of dozens of things attached to the deck, leaning to your left for an entire day, leaning to your right for an entire day, lying on a soaking-wet mattress due to a forgotten open portal, watching forgotten clothes flying off lines and into the sea, tossing waves, tossing a heavy line to someone on shore, tossing your meals to the fish, dealing with foreign immigration officers whose only English word is "no," making a note to replace the expensive camera that went overboard on a "come about," making another note in pencil to replace the expensive pen that went overboard during a "jibe," making a mental note to try to remember what was on the other notes that were soaked beyond readability when the wildcat swell roared across the deck taking with it your best friend, waiting and worrying outside the island dispensary while your best friend is stitched up by the island doctor who was kind enough to close his lobster stand to help. Yes, thank you.

May the winds be at your back, as you look from your warm, comfortable, secure living room window at all the campers, horse-back riders, fishermen, hunters, and yes, even sailors, as they head for the "grate" outdoors.

◆ ◆ ◆ What's Your Sign?

Signs have been standardized throughout the world. However, a lot of misinformation has been published about road signs, and also there are a lot of signs for which no information exists. To answer these questions about road signs, I have developed an all-inclusive list. Look it over, then take a copy with you when you travel.

Nothing is happening in this area

The sign painter ran out of paint

Number of minutes in a local hour

Keyhole capital of the world up ahead

This is the spot—dig here

 Zigzag all you want for next ten miles

 White bottles for sale

 Whatchamacallits repaired here

▲ ▲ ▲ **Who Buys It?**

Who the hell buys gifts in an airport gift shop? What kind of person knows a kind of person who is just dying for a Mexican man taking a siesta with a tall cactus growing up from between his legs? What is the thrill of buying or receiving a porcelain clock whose face and hands are only painted on? Who could live with an outline of an antique car with a wire person behind the wheel? Where would anyone put the clown holding the balloon who is being peed on by a blue-and-white dog, no less? Where is there a living room wall just crying out for a pink poodle made of puffy silk that is pressed against a field of royal-blue imitation velvet? How big a fan of Elvis do you have to be to be thrilled with a doll of him made out of beer-bottle caps? I have never seen one bedroom door on which there is glued the occupant's name on a ceramic plate. Why would anyone with an IQ even slightly above a carburetor want to buy their grandchild a T-shirt that confesses in black letters across the chest that their grandmother—YOU—went somewhere and all you got them was this lousy T-shirt? What kind of mo-mo rushes home from a trip to give his loved one an ashtray that is actually a large breast?

The only motivation, other than poor taste, I see for buying any of this crap is to get even with someone you really dislike and you want them to know it. I can't think of a better way of getting even with that co-worker you despise than to give them a brass nutcracker that works by placing the walnut between female legs and smashing it with her crotch.

Now, if by any wild chance you are one of those persons who seriously buys, gives, or loves receiving an airport store gift and are insulted by what I have written, I apologize and want to make amends. So, if you send me this book and a self-addressed envelope with postage, I shall have my book covered with a see-through lavender ceramic glaze and glued onto a bright-orange fake-silk background, framed with encrusted seashells, each of which has the name of your home state hand-painted on it in fake silver, hanging from a thirty-six-inch, pure-plated-brass link chain that would go perfectly with the peanut-shell collage of pit bulls playing shuffleboard with the collies. Or, you could hang it around your neck next to your red, white, and blue licorice American flag hanging on the chain of plated beer-can rings. I mean it, you schmuck.

◇ ◇ ◇  **Things You Hate to Hear**

The following are things you hate to hear when you are traveling:

■ "I thought *you* were listening when he was giving us directions."
■ "It isn't on the map."
■ "Are the blue lines highways or rivers?"
■ "It's not my job to awaken passengers."
■ "Daddy, Mommy, look what the dog did in the cooler."
■ "Ladies and gentlemen, this is your pilot. . . . Oh, God, how do I explain this?"
■ "Folks, in my forty-two years of piloting, I've never seen anything like this."
■ "This is your pilot. Is there anyone on board who can speak Arabic—calmly?"
■ "Ladies and gentlemen, although radar can be wrong . . ."
■ "If there is a heart specialist on board, would he please come to the cockpit."
■ "If anyone on board knows how to fly a 747, please come to the cockpit immediately."
■ "Everyone, please come to the cockpit immediately."
■ "If anyone sees where the captain is, please ask him to return to the cockpit immediately."
■ "If there is anyone on board who can keep a very big secret, please come to the cockpit immediately."
■ "Sorry, your insurance doesn't include luggage once it leaves your house."
■ "According to your policy, a 'masked holdup' is an Act of God."
■ "If you look closely, you'll see that it reads 'instant playback,' not 'instant payback.' "
■ "We found a lost bag once, I think."
■ "All the caller said was 'Thank you for the new luggage and the clothes.' "

- "Hi, we're on our honeymoon."
- "Mother can come with us after all?"
- "Do you mind if I smoke?"
- "Look at them closely. They don't read 'American Express.' They read 'Marrakesh Express.' "
- "In your money, that converts to—hold on to your hat . . ."
- "I've never seen a rash like that in my life."
- "If it had blue eyes, it's poisonous."
- "Hey, Tony, wanna laugh? They think we honor Triple A."
- "Never in my long life as a mechanic have I ever seen a transmission like this."
- "You sure you left it with us to fix?"
- "I'm also the sheriff."

★ ★ ★ **Native Dress**

One of the unique qualities of American tourists is how they return to their country wearing the native costume of the country they visited.

I saw a middle-aged couple walking in the Detroit airport toward baggage claim. The man was wearing matching shorts and shirt in a brightly colored flower print. On his head was a straw hat with small plastic pineapples hanging from the rim. His wife was decked out in a straw skirt, a flowered blouse matching her husband's shirt, and a hat woven with bamboo leaves. As they approached me, I asked, "How was Hawaii?" They were startled. "How did you know we were in Hawaii? Were you in our hotel in Waikiki?" I told them I just had a sixth sense about where people had been. They shifted their matching canvas coconut bags to their other shoulders and left.

I'm sure you know exactly what I'm talking about. As a matter of fact, you probably have a Parisian beret, a pair of leather lederhosen from Germany, and Dutch wooden shoes. The odds are about two million to one that after you walked in your house, you never put them on again.

Let me give you something to think about. Did you ever notice when you are visiting a country that you never see one native dressed in the costume you have just purchased, except for a nightclub act or the person who sold you the outfit? To better illustrate my point, imagine that you are sitting in the Tokyo airport and a 747 packed with Japanese returning from a visit to America arrives. All the Japanese men deplaning are dressed in cowboy boots with spurs, chaps, plaid shirts with string ties, leather vests with silver buttons and fringes, big silver belt buckles with a horse's head engraved on them, kerchiefs around their necks, six-guns in holsters hanging low and tied to their legs, chaws of tobacco in their cheeks, and ten-gallon hats on their heads. Their women are in leather skirts branded with buffaloes, matching leather vests over bare skin, soft moccasins, silver and turquoise belts, brightly beaded headbands, and carrying bows and arrows. Now do you get the picture?

Put down this book. Walk to a full-length mirror. Look at yourself in it. See the way you look? Well, the next time you travel outside the USA, come back home looking the same.

◆ ◆ ◆ If We Skip Lunch

Hundreds of magazine and newspaper articles have been written on how to budget for a trip. Entire books have been devoted to this one subject. I grant you that money is a major factor, but there is something way more important, and that is having the best time of your life.

I am speaking to you as someone who understands from experience what it is to not know where the next dollar is going to come from or if it is going to come. My whole life hasn't been stretch limousines and splendiferous hotel suites. More than half my time on earth has been riding on subways and sleeping in closet-size hotel rooms with a bathroom at the end of the hall. What I am about to tell you comes from my poor years, for it was back then that I thought of it and still live it.

Don't follow other people's suggestions for detailed lists of anticipated expenses: so much for baby-sitters, car rental, cigarettes, tips, hairdresser, etc. Usually this is followed by formulas for cutting back on this and saving on that. Forget about it.

Think about where you want to go. Buy the least expensive round-trip ticket on a plane, train, bus, camel, anything. Prebook a hotel room, which you can always upgrade or downgrade when you get there. Now, think of how much money you have or want to spend. Take that amount and buy traveler's checks with it. Pack your bags with what possessions you have, buying nothing new, and go there.

When you get there—do, see, feel, taste, touch, and experience all your heart desires. When you run out of money, go home, remembering that it isn't how much time you spend somewhere that makes it memorable; it's how you spend the time.

How much do you want to bet I'm right? You can pay me after you come home.

◆ ◆ ◆ The Little Darlings

If you must take your children, or anyone's children for that matter, on a long car trip, before you leave home, record yourself screaming the most often used words and expressions for taming the little darlings. This will save you a lot of time and strain, because you yell only once—into the microphone. The hardest work after that is pressing the playback button. I'm sure you can rattle off a long list of your own, but I offer you the following as a guideline.

- "Stop that!"
- "I don't care who started it."
- "How'd you like a knuckle sandwich?"
- "Give it back!"
- "Share!"
- "I don't care whose it is!"
- "If I have to stop this car, everyone is in trouble!"
- "I told you to go before we left the house!"
- "That's your problem!"
- "Take that out of the dog's nose!"
- "Take that out of your sister's nose!"
- "Take that out of your nose!"
- "Take that out of my nose!"
- "How'd you like someone to do that to you?"
- "Stop making that noise!"
- "Why didn't you tell me we left him?"
- "No, you can't!"
- "I never promised!"
- "If that gets on the seat, you're dead meat!"
- "In one minute I'm turning around and going home!"
- "In one minute I'm never going to turn around and go home!"
- "Where's Junior?"

- "You threw *what* out the window?"
- "No!"
- "Never!"
- "Over my dead body!"
- "When you grow up!"
- "How would you like to see the inside of the trunk?"
- "Soon!"
- "Stop asking!"
- "I just answered that!"
- "When I was a kid . . ."
- "Your face will freeze like that!"
- "That's how people lose an eye!"
- "I'm pulling over! Hold it in! Cup your hand!"
- "We'll clean it up at the next gas station!"
- "I have a nose!"
- "Okay, who did it?"
- "It's not funny!"
- "If I come back there, someone is dead!"
- "The following allowances are canceled . . ."
- "Another peep and it's liver for the next four nights!"
- "Pull your pants back up!"
- "Whoever's imitating the siren, knock it off!"
- "Roll up the windows!"
- "Stop kicking the seat!"
- "I can't; I'm driving!"
- "Take that off my head!"
- "Stop yelling. I see the rabbit!"
- "Stop crying!"
- "It was already dead!"
- "I'm not going back!"
- "Okay, it's buried. Satisfied?"
- "This is the last chorus of 'One Hundred Bottles of Beer on the Wall'!"
- "Close that door!"
- "Don't touch anything!"
- "Don't even think about it!"
- "I'm selling you in the next town!"
- "Enough 'Row, Row, Row Your Boat'!"

- "The highway monster hates noisy children!"
- "Look—Jason!"
- "Okay, who wants an enema?"
- "Take that out of my shirt, now!"
- "Stop! I can't see the road!"
- "Arrrrgggghhhhhhhhhh!"
- "Mercy!"
- "You were all adopted."

▼ ▼ ▼ **Not on Any Map**

Although I have traveled most of our globe, there is one place my parents, as did many parents, promised to send me many, many times that I have yet to find. If you have any information as to where it is, I'd appreciate hearing from you: where the hell is "Kingdom Come"?

▼   ▼   ▼   # What's Your Sign?

You're allowed to drive straight down or up

Percentage of literacy in next town

Top of camel crossing

Watch out for falling black shoes

Did you remember your pocket handkerchief?

No Roman numerals allowed in this area

No bugle-playing at any time

 Allowed to drive on two wheels

▲ ▲ ▲ Go or No Go?

You know, beyond any doubt, that it is a definite "no go" if a trip you are considering calls for any of the following items:

- toilet paper
- lots of extra deodorant
- surgical needle and thread
- waterproof matches
- lots of Lomotil
- a hand-held crucifix
- extra-thick gloves
- any kind of tools
- a water purifier
- your will
- a fake passport
- grandparents' birthplaces
- medical history of social diseases
- proof of religion

- hard hat
- thermal long johns
- protractor
- one wash 'n' wear condom
- next of kin's names
- reasons why you believe in reincarnation
- dissecting instruments
- blowgun
- artist's rendering of you in profile
- your lawyer's private home phone number
- your last words
- large amount of cash in small, unmarked bills
- lye
- dental records
- X ray of your lower body
- mosquito netting
- barbed-wire cutters
- plumber's tape
- garlic on a chain
- duster coat
- a llama
- a sword
- a videotape of you disowning your country
- litter box
- a copy of *Women Who Hate Men*
- a copy of *Men Who Hate Women*
- a copy of *Men Who Love Men*
- a copy of *Men Who Love Llamas*
- an extra-large pooper scooper
- fake mustache and sideburns
- earplugs
- nose plugs
- rectal plugs
- your mortgage and title papers
- callous clippers
- callous saw
- list of worst fears
- 1940 lineup of Philadelphia A's

- helmet
- small cloth doll of yourself
- signed power-of-attorney form
- bag of 1943 silver Lincoln-head pennies
- radiation-protective gear
- rubber pants
- set of conga drums
- ear-piercing tools
- a dwarf

PREPARING FOR YOUR TRIP

▶ ▶ ▶ ▶ ▶ ▶ ▶ ▶ ▶ ▶ ▶ ▶ ▶ ▶ ▶ ▶ ▶

◇　◇　◇　# You Can't Miss It

The villa I had rented in Marbella, Spain, was a headquarters from which I could visit other places. The easiest expedition, and therefore my first, was Mijas, a small, picturesque town famous for its beauty and exciting bullfights.

After a hot cup of Spanish coffee and some hearty laughs with family and friends, my traveling companion—Elizabeth—and I leapt into our fire-engine-red Alfa Romeo Spider convertible and sped out to the main highway. From there, it was a simple matter of making a left, going a few miles, then another left onto the road that leads directly to Mijas.

We looked forward to what was supposed to be one of the most beautiful scenic drives, especially in the very early morning light. The mere utterance of the name Mijas to any Spaniard or foreigner who has been there automatically elicits two responses—"Muy bonita" and "You can't miss it."

Well, I don't mean to brag, but if there is any place in the world, and I mean any place, that cannot be missed, yours truly can miss it. Without even trying, I might add. As a matter of fact, I can get lost in a driveway. Usually, the confusion about where to turn, cross, go up, go down, or back up begins two seconds after turning the key in the ignition. On my driver's license, it states that I have never gotten a ticket for speeding, I don't have to wear glasses when driving, and I am to be afforded every courtesy in helping me get to where I have been trying to get.

In spite of my history of passing over borders of countries that aren't even on the map; in spite of spending the greater part of a day and a vacation peering at a map and then seeing how many pieces it can be ripped into; in spite of wanting to buy a summer house directly next door to my home, so I wouldn't risk getting lost on weekends; in spite of these and thousands of other reasons why a steering wheel should never be in my hands unless I am picking it up off the ground, I always begin every trip full of confidence.

I have visited and driven in dozens of countries, every state except Alaska, literally hundreds of cities and towns, and I have gotten lost in every single one of them. This even includes my hometown of Philadelphia. Hell, let me be one hundred percent honest: I used to get lost in my own neighborhood. When I made it to the end of my block, my neighbors applauded.

The state that is the worst offender in my opinion is New Jersey. I swear, the whole state looks the same to me. I think they have seven people and nine trees and they keep moving them down the road. Then there are the Jersey traffic circles. Once you get into them, you can't get out. You keep driving around endlessly. I've seen 1929 Fords with skeletons at the wheel whipping around those circles.

For most confusing city, although Rome and Paris are strong contenders, first prize has to go to Los Angeles. In any other city in the world, if you should happen to make a mistake while at the wheel, you can get off the highway and then maneuver your way back on. You get on any of those freeways in L.A. and make one little mistake, you're in Guam.

Any small town in the U.S. can be a terror, but the trophy goes to any small town in the Deep South. The people living there are among the most considerate and helpful citizens in our country. They always want to help. Matter of fact, dead people in the Deep South leap out of their graves just to give directions. However, you know there are regional differences in the way we talk in America. Sometimes, it's amazing that we Americans are all able to communicate with one another at all—and one of those sometimes is definitely when I'm behind the wheel of a car, and lost. As hard as I try to understand what is being told me, I can't. First of all, regardless of where I am, once directions involve more than three turns, they start to sound like a prayer to me:

"You go to the corner, make a left, take a right at the next street, a sharp left at the supermarket, and then you *domini dominus dominatio respecto Christo* . . ."

"Thank you, Father."

Getting back to the small town in the Deep South. When you ask directions, the dialogue always goes something like this:

"Excuse me, sir . . ." I always call the person I'm asking directions sir. He could be standing there picking his nose with a broom. "How do I get back on I-95?"

"You asked the right person, sonny. I-95 is my specialty. You can't miss it, no sirree, Bob."

"Oy."

"Just go up yonder a piece."

"A piece of what?"

"It's about a whoop and a holler."

"I don't think I have enough gas for both."

"And make a left at the house where Elmer Bodie died."

"Elmer's dead? I'll be dipped."

My first driving experience in the South was a disaster. I don't know how I did it, but somehow I got off Route #1 and was on Dust Bowl Back Road #0. It was one of those blistering hot Georgia July afternoons. I could smell rubber burning and it was coming from the bottom of my sneakers. A desert had sneaked into my throat. I felt as if I were trying to swallow a dozen hair balls. Then, through the shimmering heat rising from the road, I saw it: a sign. A big sign. Relief. TEN MILES TO STUCKEY'S.

I floored the accelerator, with images of frozen lime juice and extra-thick milkshakes before my eyes. Another sign, bigger: SIX MILES TO STUCKEY'S.

I pressed my left foot on top of my right foot, feeling the iced tea with lemon cascading down my parched throat. An even bigger sign appeared: STUCKEY'S TWO MILES.

I drove the next two miles standing up, my head pressed against the hot roof of my car, screaming at the top of my red-hot lungs: "Come on, Stuckey's! Lay it—no, *pour* it on me! Stuckey's, baby!"

The next and last billboard was gigantic. AROUND THE NEXT BEND—STUCKEY'S.

I whipped around the next bend doing about ninety miles per hour on one and one-half wheels, and there she was— S-T-U-C-K-E-Y'-S! A small roadside stand, smaller than my backseat, that sold more than one hundred different edibles made out of dry, sugar-coated pecans. Sugar-coated pecans—the perfect thirst quencher.

Another time, I got it real good in a small town. I still can't believe I fell for it. But you know how sometimes, for some reason, maybe just the fact that we are surrounded by lots of bricks and concrete, we big-city dwellers make the mistake of thinking that we are smarter than small-town folks. That in itself should prove just how stupid we big-city folks are.

Anyway, unless the population had decreased overnight by 99.9 percent, I was lost in a small town. I looked for a normal person to ask for directions. I found one.

Now, maybe it was my big-city, Eastern accent or the way I was dressed or simply his idea of humor, but when I asked him how to get back on the main highway leading to the city, he replied, "It's real easy. All y'all do is go to the last stop sign and make a right."

It was so simple, I wanted to kiss him, but instead I just thanked him enthusiastically and followed the easy directions. Forty-five minutes later, I thought, "How do you know when you are at the *last* stop sign?" It was a miracle I didn't drive to Alaska.

I hate asking for directions anywhere, anytime, but especially when a woman is in the car with me. It must be part of that damn male ego that makes all men not want to admit that they are doing anything wrong. Admit to a woman that I'm lost? I'd rather have my left hand suddenly change into a foot. In my mind, I can hear her thinking, "Dumb, David; dumb, David." So, no matter what I do, I make believe it is part of my plan. I could drive straight off a cliff: "Why are you screaming? I know exactly what I'm doing. I do it all the time. As soon as we hit the bottom, I make a sharp left."

Another thing that bugs me is that when I finally concede that I'm lost and stop and ask someone for directions, his first reply is almost always, "Huh?"

The worst place to ask for directions is a gas station. First of all, did you ever notice that the same guy works in every gas station in this country? It's that guy with the hunting jacket and earmuffs. Of course, in July, he turns the muffs up. And he wipes your windshield with that same filthy, black rag, which I am convinced is being mailed from station to station. His directions always start with, "Okay, buddy, pull out of the station."

"No, I want to drive around your pumps for a few hours. I don't want to pull out of the station."

Then he gives you the map treatment.

"You're right here."

And his hand covers New York, Colorado, and Wyoming.

Here's something else I've never been able to figure out. How come maps have to be so big? Why does everyone have to get out of the car in order to open the map?

"Jump out, I'm opening the map. I'll pick you up at the next corner."

And just once in my lifetime, I'd like to be able to fold a map back to its original creases. After I open and fold back eight or nine maps, everyone in the car has to take a bus to our destination.

People in my hometown of Philadelphia give great directions, because nearly everything in town is named after Benjamin Franklin.

"Go down Benjamin Franklin Parkway, past the Benjamin Franklin Museum, take a right at the Benjamin Franklin Motel. You can't miss it. It's shaped like a kite and has a large key hanging from it."

New York City people give the best directions in America. They're always the same and you can always understand them.

"Excuse me. Could you tell me how to get to Times Square?"

"Go to hell! Whadda I look like, a goddamn information booth or somethin'?"

"Thank you very much."

"Thank this, pal. I got your thanks right here!"

The best Big Apple directions story I know is about a fellow Philadelphian who was driving to the city to go to a recording studio in Manhattan. All he remembered was that it was near the Americana Hotel. He could find it from there, so when he pulled alongside a well-dressed businessman carrying an expensive attaché, he rolled down his car window and spoke to him in his friendliest tone of voice.

"Excuse me, sir. Could you please tell me how to get to the Americana Hotel?"

The successful New Yorker, meticulously dressed in a three-piece suit, silver streaks running along his well-groomed hair, looked directly into the inquiring face and exclaimed, "Fuck you! Sleep in Jersey!"

Where was I? What was I telling you about? See, even when I *write* about driving, I get lost. . . . Oh, yeah, the drive to Mijas. So, I made a left on the main highway, and when I saw a sign announcing that Mijas was the next left, I took the next left. You couldn't drive more than one hundred yards without seeing a big billboard advertising that weekend's bullfight in Mijas. This had to be the right road. I mean, when the Mets are playing at home, all the billboards announcing the game are . . . are . . . all over the city, the suburbs, on every highway leading into the city . . . shit!

Directly ahead was a town. Well, not exactly a town. It was a town that was being built, a soon-to-be town. I was lost. I drove up and down the soon-to-be-paved streets in the soon-to-be town for about thirty minutes. Workers began waving to me the second and third time I whipped by them. I smiled, making believe I was interested in buying a soon-to-be house in the soon-to-be town. It wasn't working, especially for Elizabeth, who had been in enough cars with me to know I was lost and to know also that to mention it was to invite murder. Even though I knew she knew, I acted as though she didn't know, and I knew she knew I was only acting as if she didn't know.

One hour and thirty-seven soon-to-be houses later, I stopped the car and got out. I had no choice. I had to go to the bathroom. I walked around to the other side of a dirt mound and started to relieve myself. What a beautiful view. Such wonderful fields. Such a quaint town over there, such a . . . even from this distance, Mijas looked exactly as it did on the brochure.

We were there fifteen minutes later. Mijas was all that it was hyped to be, and I felt that having dinner and watching the sunset, instead of the original plan of breakfast and shopping, was much better. I don't know if Elizabeth would agree. I never asked her, because she is too nice to kill.

The obvious question is, why, if I always get lost and have fits when I do, do I ever get behind the wheel of a car? The answer is also obvious: because I love to drive.

▼ ▼ ▼ # What's Your Sign?

Ski caps for sale

Watch out for people without feet, hands, and necks

Billiard room up ahead

Jugglers wanted

Verboten to chase children

Hold it in—sorry

Do whatever you want. Who the hell cares?

People with children only

Things You'll Never See When You Are Traveling

- A smile on the face of everyone working behind the ticket counter.

- A foreign airport in which everyone doesn't look as if they are escaping from an invading army that is advancing on their city.

- Someone stopped at airport security who actually has a weapon or bomb.

- A good-looking person at the Reno bus station.

- Everyone in the station actually waiting for a bus.

- A vending machine in a bus station without kick marks.

- The name of a cabdriver you can actually pronounce.

- A cabdriver who looks something like the picture on his cab license.

- Everything you ordered from room service, exactly as you ordered it.

- A preordered breakfast at the time indicated.

- Understandable and easy-to-follow hotel fire-escape instructions.

- No four-letter words scratched into the brass doors of an elevator.

- A maître d' with his hands in his pockets when he leads you to your table.

- A nun traveling alone.

- Only people you'd like to see nude at a nude beach.

- A Japanese tourist looking at something without taking a picture of it.

- An American airport, bus station, or train depot not littered with beer and soda bottles and cans and paper.

- An American beach not littered with beer and soda bottles and cans and paper.

◆ ◆ ◆ **A Pack Rat**

Almost everyone overpacks. The most familiar excuse is "Suppose we get there and need it?" A close second is "Suppose we can't get this over there?" I have had an independent company conduct a survey of the most useless items taken on trips over the past year. Never once, by one person, for one second, were any of the following used. An amazing 96 percent of the items were never even removed from their suitcases. You can be assured that by checking this list, you won't pack any absolutely unnecessary items, or anything that could get you into trouble. Never, ever pack:

Any kind of small, irregular animal.

A book of 1,001 terrorist jokes.

Your Triple A membership card, because chances are that Arlo, the owner of the garage in the town where your car breaks down, won't know how to spell it, let alone know what it is.

Nude pictures of Yogi Berra.

The Polaroid pictures you and your lover took that night you were feeling silly and sexy and had that sheep outfit and cat-o'-nine-tails.

A list of things you would do were you elected President.

A list of things you would do if Quayle were elected President.

The ol' college recipe for brownies.

Extra passport pictures in each of which you look like someone else.

False teeth that don't belong to you.

Fake chest hair.

A three-cupped bra.

A bottle of Flintstone vitamins when you're not with a child.

Lock-picking device.

Animal pelts.

More than one kilo of mashed potatoes.

A book on how to grow mushrooms.

The ol' college recipe for mushrooms.

A three-piece, fire-engine-red suit with matching shoes.

An extra, extra, extra large jockstrap.

A Polaroid picture of you wearing above jockstrap on your head.

Anything that will be out of style next year when your bag is returned.

Anything that, God forbid, if you don't make it back, will be an embarrassment to you even in the next world.

▶ ▶ ▶ # Don't Fly It; Fly It

I discovered the perfect prevention of lost baggage. I've been doing it for about a year now. I've been ecstatic! It has been worth every dime it has cost me. Not only have I eliminated the worry of losing a bag when I fly, I no longer have to lift or carry it, either. When I say perfect, I mean perfect.

Well, just today, I was expressing my happiness over this system with my manager, Steve, who asked me a simple question.

"Do you know how Federal Express sends your bag?"

"I never asked. How?"

"By plane."

WANTED: Young person, strong of back, trustworthy, enjoys great outdoors, loves to walk great distances in the USA and internationally, capable of swimming transoceanic, to hand-carry and deliver celebrity's baggage. Send résumé and personal references (*NOT BY AIRMAIL*).

▼ ▼ ▼ People Lie, Not Numbers

One of the most reliable factors in scientific analysis is numerical evidence. The same is true of travel. When we know the statistics on how many persons are and are not doing this or that, or the odds against this or that happening, we are creating for the traveler a true, right-on-target, no-holds-barred, no-BS look into the matter.

The following is not guesswork, but numerical truths covering many important aspects of your next trip, whether it is for pleasure or business. You are about to become a very well-informed traveler, thanks to the world of cold, hard facts:

Only 17.2% of Americans have been to Maine, as compared to 37.6% of the people from Maine having been to America.

Every 10.5 minutes, someone in a public pool is asking themselves, "Why should I get out of the pool to go to the bathroom?"

98.1% of those who do not leave the pool to go to the bathroom do a Number One.

90.4% of airline mechanics travel by bus, 6.8% by car, and 2.8% walk.

90.6% of insects and 74.5% of vegetation directly below you die when you squat in the woods to go to the bathroom.

Only 1.1% of people squatting in the woods to go to the bathroom are killed by insects or vegetation directly below them.

One out of five illegal aliens who are sent back to their country has been tipped by you.

Only one out of one hundred illegal aliens who are sent back to their countries bother to change clothes before slipping back into the USA.

If you increase your car's speed to 90.2 mph while your dog has his head out the window, his tongue will fly out of his ass at the exact speed of the car.

When you are given directions, the odds are 1,000,245 to 1 in favor of your hearing harp music and seeing naked TV repairmen dancing on huge, seedless red grapes over your remembering the directions.

If the Disney characters' heads were actually that big in comparison to their bodies in real life, 100% of their mothers would have exploded during childbirth.

When a man in the hills of the Deep South calls his wife "Ma," the odds are four to one she is.

If you were to lay every New York hooker end to end, it would cost you $1,245,500.

37.5% of the world's population understands and speaks English as opposed to .02% of New York City cabdrivers.

You can count the number of aviation near-misses on one hand, providing you have 1,254,780 fingers on that hand.

When you ask directions in the Midwest and Southwest, 97.4% of the time you'll be told to make a turn "Near the old Johnsons' place."

If Abraham Lincoln were actually the size of the Lincoln Memorial, his prostate would be the size of a Dodge Charger.

95.5% of the Quakers you pass on the highway have never been to Las Vegas.

37.8% of the people living in Poland think they are living in Spain.

If Disneyland were ever to sink, an artificial reef, 3.4 miles long by 2.1 miles wide, would be created by floating lens caps off Japanese cameras.

During an actual emergency, 15.8% of airplane passengers throw up in their oxygen mask and put the airsick bag over their nose and mouth.

.006% of people who put on an oxygen mask actually breathe normally.

55.5% of all comedians cannot get the oxygen mask over their noses.

The odds are 250,000 to 1 that, if your car trip is farther than one city block from your house, you will hear a child say, "Are we there yet?"

If your car stalls on railroad tracks, the odds are 6 to 1 the Amtrak will derail before it reaches you.

The inside of the bulletproof glass of the Popemobile is capable of holding 6,748 Garfield dolls.

58.6% of the time that the Loch Ness Monster is spotted nowadays, Elvis is seen riding on its back.

On an average of 2.2 times per week, Greek vandals try to fix the ruins.

98.5% of persons who wrote you "Wish you were here" were ecstatic that you weren't.

Mexican drinking water is only 42.6% as effective a laxative as being more than one hundred miles from home and hearing a car mechanic utter the two words "new transmission."

When in an airplane crash, it is 100% unnecessary to place your head in your crotch, because at the descending G-force, your crotch will come up to your head.

A fat person getting off an airplane toilet seat makes a sound ten times greater than that of 14,005 Garfield dolls being simultaneously popped off a sheet of plate glass the size of Vermont.

In the entire history of Disneyland, not one person has been flashed during the playing of "It's a Small World."

48.6% of all Italian tourists driving in the USA, upon seeing the NO U-TURNS sign, feel they are being singled out.

When people are stuck in traffic in back of a horse's behind sticking out of a horse trailer, 48.6% report thinking of their boss, 49.8% of the President, and 1.6% think naughty thoughts.

Nine out of ten salmon who are taught to drive a motor vehicle drive against traffic.

When a person weighing more than 250 pounds gets into a car, the cat sleeping under it will be crushed to death within 2.3 seconds.

78.9% of persons who reach the line "Thou shalt not steal" written in the hotel-room Gideon Bible are reading it while in their homes.

Once every 37.6 seconds, an international flight attendant somewhere is demonstrating how to put on the oxygen mask without actually putting it on for fear of messing her hair.

In actual emergencies, 23.4% of women also do not put on the oxygen mask for fear of messing their hair, even if their hair is being singed.

96.5% of the 23.4% are Jewish women.

27.8% of all Polish female passengers put on an oxyen mask for absolutely no reason.

If given the choice, 96.2% of children would not put an oxygen mask over their parents' noses and mouths in a real emergency.

Every 30.4 seconds a male camper somewhere who has had more than four beers is saying, "I'll show you how to put out a campfire."

In eight out of ten cases of a father coming out of a coma after a family barbecue, the last words he remembers hearing are "Roll, Dad, roll!"

Seven out of ten toll collectors listed as their biggest annoyance "knowing that people can see up their nostrils."

Upon seeing a road-repair worker waving a fluorescent orange flag, 98.8% of drivers think or exclaim, "I don't believe they're getting seventeen dollars an hour to do that!"

99.5% of the people who lock their luggage with those teensy-weensy keys also believe that no one can break into their locked diaries.

98.1% of persons stranded in an airport longer than 6.2 hours are plotting an average of 7.5 murders, and 100% of the potential victims are wearing airline uniforms.

If you tie a harmonica to your hood ornament and go 62.6 mph around a corner at a 30.7° angle, you will play the song "Glow-worm."

1.6% of car owners believe that "station wagon" spelled backward is "No, a tit wags on."

In any area of the United States, if a man and a dog are struck simultaneously by a moving vehicle, 97.6% of all people would help the dog first.

In the above situation, 98.7% of dogs would help the man.

When you see a car anywhere in the USA with a pair of fur dice hanging from the rearview mirror, or one door or fender not the same color as the others, the odds are 15,550 to 1 that someone in the car is an illegal alien.

When you see a teenage minority-group member driving a car

costing more than $35,000, the odds are 5,250 to 1 that the product he sells to make his living cannot be spread on bread, baked in a microwave, or used openly in public.

You have to honk a car horn an average of 5.8 minutes before the workers inside the state road-crew truck awaken.

It requires two persons an average of 3.7 hours to refold a road map.

On every map there is an average of six red, two black, and four blue lines that have absolutely no bearing whatsoever to the topography, road system, or river locations of the particular area in question.

Only one in every 8,240 Americans is able to read a road map, and only one in every 16,639 Americans is able to follow a road map.

98.4% of road-map makers have tested in the top 95.2 percentile of sadism.

Every year in the United States, an average of 8,784 divorces are caused by arguments over road maps.

A road map will disappear from view in 3.2 seconds when thrown from the window of a car going 55 mph.

In 84.6% of the cases in Italy, if a nun has a severe sunburn and you slap her on the back and say, "How you doing, sister?" she will yell, "You son of a bitch!"

After a straight run of 18.6 hours on a bus, your rear end is so numb that it is legal to perform surgery on it without using anesthesia.

85.6% of people surveyed who had gone to the bathroom on a bus said that it didn't bother them at all that there was no bathroom on the bus.

The odds are nine out of ten that within 4.6 minutes after leaving your car in a garage in the South, the mechanic will put your old radiator hose between his legs and say, "Hey, Arlo, check it out!"

If you were to moon out of the sunroof of a car going 87.6 mph, you would play the whistling theme from the movie *The Good, the Bad and the Ugly*.

98.3% of all people will believe any statistic that is an odd number, such as 98.3%, versus an even number, such as 98%, or 7.6 inches versus 7 inches, 58.2 miles versus 58 miles, et cetera, which is why 87.3% of Americans don't believe there are exactly 10,000 lakes in Minnesota, but were they to claim 10,174 lakes, then 100.8% of Americans would take it as gospel. The next time you have a free 10.6 minutes, think about it.

▼ ▼ ▼ # What's Your Sign?

They went thataway

Sorry—thataway

Only people dressed all in white allowed

One left-handed glove for sale ahead

Only emphatic statements allowed

Go left, go right, go left, go right, go left

Obey walking backward up stairs law

Listen for fox-hunt bugle signal

▲ ▲ ▲ Enough Is More Than Enough

Place two pieces of luggage on your bed. In the first one, pack everything you could not do without on your trip, such as birth control pills, prescription drugs and medicines, a spare pair of reading glasses, charge cards, passport, visas, traveler's checks, international driver's license, address book, Eurorailpass, and airline tickets. Next put in those personal, irreplaceable items that even the thought of losing would kill you, such as your wedding picture, final divorce papers, Elvis' autograph, and your pet's picture. Now, close the bag.

Now, open the second bag and fill it with all the things you want to have on your trip but aren't absolutely essential and could be replaced, if necessary, such as a change or two of underwear, last year's Christmas present, a tube of Ben-Gay, and the robe your mate loves. Now, close the bag.

Okay, now, bag number one is your carry-on bag for the plane, and bag number two is to be left on the bed for you to unpack when you return home. This way, you don't have to worry about lost luggage or overpacking. You're welcome.

◇ ◇ ◇ Child Prevention

Children on trips are like hemorrhoids; even if they are perfect, they are a pain in the ass. If you are presently single or married without children and think I am exaggerating the impact children have on vacationing adults, I can only suggest that you borrow a niece or nephew, or a neighbor's child, and take them with you. Children should be left at home, but this can be psychologically traumatic, unless, of course, it is their idea to remain. So . . .

Casually say, "There are wonderful children's dentists in Maui, darling."

Have menus printed from places you'll be staying that list only the foods your child abhors. With just a little thought, you'd be surprised how easily you can create over twenty dishes made with liver.

If you know the name of the class schmuck, mention the coincidence that he and your child's schoolteacher are going to be at your vacation spot. Add how much fun they'll have playing together and maybe even get a jump start on their studies. Bring home a vacation present of lots of pens and notebooks.

Stories of vicious animals, monsters, and supernatural things will turn a child on, not off, nowadays. Thank you, Hollywood. However, ugly, crawling, biting, stinging insects can still do the trick. Look at a few species from where you are going under a microscope—perfect for Show and Torture.

Disneyland and Disney World are the enemy. Airlines with their discounts for children are the enemy. Hiring a midget to dress as Mickey Mouse and attempt to eat your family pet right in front of your child, then showing stock air-crash footage, should help you defeat the enemy.

However, as strongly as I believe children should be left at home, I also believe that when children become adults, it is also their duty to take their parents on vacation with them. Don't you agree?

★ ★ ★ # Too Long, Too Often

You know you've been traveling too long or too often, if, *when you are home,* you do any of the following:

- Pack a bag when you are not going anywhere.
- Steal the towels out of your own bathroom.
- Put your shoes outside your bedroom door.
- Wake up in your bed, pick up your phone, and dial 164 for room service.
- Leave a tip on your dining-room table.
- Look for a stranger standing next to you in your bathroom.
- Wait in the hall of your home for an elevator.
- Put a CLEAN ROOM sign on your bedroom doorknob.
- Nail the lamps and TV-channel switcher to tables.
- Pick up the phone and dial your own phone number.
- Search the house for the "What To Do" magazine.
- Tip your spouse for cleaning your bedroom.
- When pouring a drink, you go into the hall to find the ice machine.
- When finishing a bad meal, you decide never to eat there again.
- Ask any woman you hear speaking Spanish to give you extra towels.
- After finishing a meal, lean the dining-room table up against the wall in its original upright takeoff and landing position.
- Point out emergency exits in your house to guests.
- Watch your TV for departure and arrival times.
- Constantly have the strong feeling you've been here before.
- Throw the car from drive into reverse to see what'll happen, forgetting you're in your own car, not a rental.
- Write down your own mileage when getting out of your car.
- Wear a "Hello. My name is . . ." tag.
- Get upset to see no sanitation strip across your toilet.

- Can't understand, when returning to your place, why it hasn't been cleaned while you were gone for the day.
- When bumping into a friend, you ask them what they are doing there.

◆ ◆ ◆ Only the Scenery

About six weeks before a vacation starts, I start worrying about what clothes to take. I begin putting outfits and incidentals in a closet I call my "trip closet." I always overdo it. Anyone looking in my trip closet would conclude that I am about to visit Venus and Neptune, after a short stop in each of the fifty states. Why else would there be a pile of bathing suits on top of a pile of ski sweaters, which are next to the tank tops and desert boots?

As the years and trips passed, my confusion concerning travel wardrobe worsened. It had to end. But how? If only I could create an all-purpose wardrobe. Then the only planning question would be "how much" rather than "what." It definitely would require interchangeable clothing. And wouldn't it be fantastic if everything could be purchased in one store? I dedicated myself to the solution. After a lot of thought and deductive reasoning, I figured it out.

In one afternoon, in one Banana Republic store, I purchased everything anyone would need on any trip anywhere at any time of the year. I mean *everything!* All the clothing was interchangeable because there were only earth tones: khaki, olive, cream, beige, and off-white. Therefore, every shirt went with every pair of pants, both of which were matched with the socks, with every rain jacket, with every belt and tie. It all would have gone with every hat, too, but I don't wear hats because I look like a schmuck in them.

From then on, a few days before a vacation was to begin, I would go into my *new and improved* trip closet and put together whatever was needed in a matter of a few minutes, literally. I wore this wonderful, all-purpose wardrobe on several sailing trips in the Caribbean, aboard a private motor yacht cruise along the coasts of France and Italy, a thirty-day stay on the French Riviera, a long weekend in London, a week in Hawaii, four days relaxing on the west coast of Florida, six days in Miami, a week in the Bahamas, sailing cruises to Turkey and Greece, and aboard luxury ocean liners to Yugoslavia, Italy, Malta, Portugal, and Central and South America.

How's that for validation? Imagine all these various environments, during all times of the year, and with only one wardrobe. The perfect solution to the what-to-take problem. It would have remained perfect if I hadn't looked through the photo albums one night. There I was in all these wonderful places wearing the same damn clothes. I always looked the same. Only the scenery changed. It was as though I had gone to some photo store and had taken pictures in front of scenery flats. An earth-tone schmuck.

Now, whenever anyone notices the similarity in the photos, I simply tell them that they are from the year I took off to see the world. But I'll tell you something. After these past few years of going crazy picking out what to wear on the trips I've taken, I am just about ready for another super shopping spree in Banana Republic. Last time I passed by one, I noticed they have some blue and yellow pants, which I could also get in earth tones, but they don't go together, so maybe if I buy only off-white shirts and take a black belt, but that's too dark for tropical places, so maybe I should buy . . .

▸ ▸ ▸ # Home Secure Home

One of my greatest fears is that while I'm away, my home will be robbed. This is in spite of the fact that my windows are bulletproof, my locks are the best money can buy, my burglar alarm system is the most sophisticated in the world, my German shepherd attack dog weighs one hundred and thirty pounds, an armed guard lives in a basement apartment, and I live within gunshot of a precinct of New York's finest. Still, I worry. So, I have developed a list of other things you and I can do to secure our homes, so we can rest easy while we are gone.

- A dummy of thief climbing in your window. First come, first rob.
- Realistic mannequin hanging by neck that is easily seen from living-room window.
- Leave house in total disarray so it looks as though it has already been ransacked.
- Gunpowder keg on front stoop with wires attached to it and leading under door with ticking sound emanating from inside.
- Tape of tough voice saying, "Try it, you dumb S.O.B., and you're dead meat!"
- Outside door, chalk outline of two bodies holding burglar tools.
- Sign on door: ON VACATION. COME IN. STEAL WHAT YOU WANT AND THEN TRY TO GET OUT.
- Have door knocker made from human skull.
- Surround your house with piles of cow dung.
- Put marquee outside house that reads *Ishtar*.
- Most people, including thieves, are leery of Satan-Worshiping Skinhead Transsexual Cross-Dressing Homosexual Lesbians, so put a sign outside house: GERALDO RIVERA GUESTHOUSE.

- Crooks tend to leave other crooks alone, as part of professional courtesy, so on mailbox put name of congressman.
- Put sign on lawn: EXPERIMENTAL RADON GAS, CHEMICAL WASTE DUMP-SITE, ASBESTOS HOME.
- Have bullet holes coming *out* of your front door.
- Have bloodstains running out from under your door onto your BEWARE OF PIT BULL welcome mat.
- Another sign: A PRIZE TO ANYONE WHO CAN OPEN A DOOR OR WINDOW WITHOUT GETTING THEIR HANDS AND FACE BLOWN OFF.
- Leave window shade up so one can clearly see on kitchen table a half-dead rat between two slices of rye bread.
- Leave handwritten note on front door that reads: "Sarge. Went to get beer. Rest of guys from 101st inside. Be right back. Lt. Calley."
- Put sign on door: ALL FORMS OF MARTIAL ARTS TAUGHT. SEE NINJA INSIDE.
- Leave note on front door: "Dear Thief. Hidden somewhere inside is a needle with the AIDS virus on it. Turn the knob. Ha ha ha."
- Leave all money and valuables on kitchen floor under pile of dog doo.
- Put sign on front lawn: SNAKES FOR SALE. INQUIRE INSIDE, CAREFULLY.
- Leave a recording playing on a loop of whispered conversation.
- Within entranceway, place first-prize trophies for such activities as sharpshooting, karate, kick boxing, blow-dart championship, and best detective of the century.
- On outside of doors and windows wrap police murder-investigation tape and don't forget to put the DO NOT ENTER tape in an X on your front door. You know, just like in the movies.
- Leave a dozen burnt-out crosses on your front lawn.
- Have floodlights pointing toward your house and on lawn place sign: UNFURNISHED SAMPLE HOME.
- If you live in an apartment, put a lawn in the hall and do any of the aforementioned signs.
- Leave note on door: "Neighbors have lots more than we do."
- Leave real safe in center of living room and surround it with twenty fake ones.
- Leave laundry bag near front door hanging out of which is part of a dirty policeman's uniform.

- Put condemned notice on front door.
- Brick in all doors and windows and then put fake doors and windows on outside of brick.
- Finally, rent, do not buy, your house or apartment, rent all your furniture, lease your car, rent or lease all your belongings, and even put another family's pictures in your family photo album, then go away without caring about anything that could happen.

Things You'll Never Hear

When you are traveling, you will never hear any of the following:

- I'll be more than happy to rewrite your ticket.
- We're arriving way ahead of time and there is an available gate.
- I will personally find your luggage and then personally bring it to your hotel.
- I could never describe the kick I get out of helping people.
- Wait. Your suitcase looks a little damaged. Let me give you a new one.
- It is totally our fault.
- If there's no room in the closet, I'll wear your coat during the flight so it doesn't get wrinkled.
- Our computers are not down.
- They are holding your connecting flight until you arrive.
- For all standby passengers, we are bringing in another plane.
- Flight attendant, everything was delicious.
- What an enjoyable flight. Just the right amount of air was coming out of the nozzle above me.
- Because we are so late arriving, and the food was macabre, and the toilets weren't working, and we almost crashed, and the attendants were bitchy, and it was all our fault, everyone will receive a personal letter of apology and a sizable rebate. We really love you.
- Please take your time coming up the stairs.
- This wasn't a regular stop, but I was glad to pick you up there.
- Take all the time you want to look around before returning to the tour bus.
- Don't you dare try to get out of my cab until I come around and open the door for you.
- Here, let me help you put your packages in the backseat.
- If I go too fast for you, just let me know and I'll slow down.
- Would you like me to turn down the music?
- I haven't blown my horn in over four years.
- Excuse me, sir, but you did cut in front of me back there.
- Oh, my gosh, I think I hear a squeak.
- I know a real shortcut to your hotel that will save you a mint.

HELPFUL FACTS & TIPS

▼ ▼ ▼ ▼ ▼ ▼ ▼ ▼ ▼ ▼ ▼

▼ ▼ ▼ Two Fat, Bald Women

I hate money. Wait a minute. What I actually mean is that I hate foreign money. No, that isn't true either. Okay, what I hate is trying to figure out what foreign money is worth in our money. I can never distinguish the big bills from the small bills, not in size, but in value. As a result, besides the frustrations, whenever I buy anything from anyone while anywhere in the world, I am positive I am being taken. Now, don't start telling me about calculators and electronic, pocket-size currency-exchange translators, because I hate anything with wires that is smarter than I am.

So, what I do is think of foreign money in terms of pictures. For example, I'll buy the jacket, if it costs no more than the blue bill with the castle on it and two of the fat-bald-women bills, but I will not spend two castles and the guy with the funny, droopy mustache. I'll get a pocket handkerchief for the jacket, if I can get it for the ugly woman wearing the crown and one skinny knight on horseback.

Believe it or not, one time I got my hands on a signed Dalí print for only one white-haired man on the donkey, one farmer's wife, two old orange bridges, six stacks of hay behind nine green guys with swords, and I even got two red men with big noses and three hunting dogs sitting by the fireplace in change. In American money, that would only be approximately fifteen men with the high forehead and fur-collar jacket, three guys with the mop of wavy white hair, two guys looking to their left with the ruffled shirt, and one man with the beard, big nose, and humongous ears. A real bargain, huh?

↟ ↟ ↟ Tales of the Very Old Wives

Someone, somewhere, for some reason, somehow tells someone something that isn't true, and that someone tells someone else, who tells someone, and before you know it, the lie is believed to be the gospel truth by everyone, including the someone who made it up in the first place. Well, travel has more than its share of believed untruths, and now, for the first time ever, here is a complete list of such "facts," many of which will shock you, for you have trusted them for so many years.

It is *not, absolutely not,* true . . .

- if you eat in a restaurant in Mexico, the government will reimburse you for damaged car seats.
- the money you give to religious groups in airports is sent to God on a biweekly basis.
- the literal translation of "Hari Krishna, Krishna Hari" is "Money Sucker, Sucker Money."
- you can tell the male Hari Krishnas from the female by the way their four hairs lie—left is female.
- if a child goes to the bathroom before you leave the house, they

won't have to go again until you stop for the night or for thirty feet, whichever comes first.
- gasoline station sinks are actually white.
- by law, hotel housekeepers must be as wide as their carts.
- it is a housekeepers' union rule that guests are to be awakened for "room check."
- every time you flush the toilet in your room, the ice machine in the hall fills.
- ice machines have to be as noisy as cement mixers or the ice will not be that special oblong shape.
- oblong-shaped ice tastes better than square cubes or chipped.
- the single shoes on the highways come from DC-10's.
- if you get sucked out of a plane, the distance you travel on your own will be added to your frequent-flier miles.
- when a very fat person gets stuck on an airplane, bus, or train toilet, the vapor lock caused by this will collapse the lungs of the passengers.
- the 7-Elevens are an international company, which explains why no one who works there understands English.
- airport security personnel in the USA purposely talk with each other and don't pay attention to passengers or their carry-on bags, in order to give hijackers a false sense of security.
- just because you got your eleven-inch hunting knife through airport security, it doesn't mean the American security system isn't the best.
- the reason the United States government has never done anything to free American hostages is because it would blow the cover on a very important covert action about to take place in Grenada.
- when an airline loses your luggage, they don't do everything in their power, including military force, to retrieve your luggage.
- baggage handlers try on your clothes.
- the firehose in hotels is not attached to anything.
- when you drive through a redwood tree in California, a gynecologist retires.
- after airline mechanics work on a plane, they always have unidentified parts left over.
- someone, somewhere, has a photo taken in Disneyland in which there are no Japanese.

- if a voodoo ventriloquist slaps a dummy in the head, a toll-booth collector somewhere gets a headache.
- if you give someone who is choking the Heimlich maneuver backward, you will save his life, but his ass will explode.
- when you see a businessman on a trip with his wife, she is his wife.
- men very often travel to Las Vegas with their young, gorgeous, sexy daughters.
- toll-booth collectors are wearing pants.
- you have to drive on the opposite side of the lawn when using a lawn mower in Great Britain.
- the Puerto Ricans living in New York are not the same Puerto Ricans who are living in Puerto Rico.
- the Israelis living in New York and Los Angeles are not the same Israelis who are living in Israel.
- the Eskimos living in Newark are the same as the Eskimos living in Alaska.
- the Lincoln Memorial crotch weighs more than one ton dripping wet.
- for overseas flights, no new flight attendants have been hired since 1960.
- the Mile High Club is actually a secret flight attendants' organization working undercover to free our hostages.
- travel agents really care how your trip went and really want you to stop by and tell them all about it, and not because they hope to sucker you out of more money on your next vacation.
- when the computer is down, the computer is down.
- you will never see the person who gave you directions within ten minutes after you drive away.
- conventioneers are just acting like drunks and assholes.
- if conventioneers didn't wear names on their suits, they wouldn't remember their names and would wander the earth aimlessly.
- inside every businessman is a man in a jogging suit and dirty sneakers just waiting to get out.
- if you are wearing Bermuda shorts when flying over the Bermuda Triangle, your ass will become three-sided and grow into a point.
- if you are wearing Bermuda shorts when flying over the Bermuda Triangle, your ass will disappear.

- service industries have improved remarkably in the United States since the liberalization of immigration laws.
- conventioneer name badges will be worth a fortune someday.
- if you see the rivets popping out of the wing of a plane while in flight, you will someday be saying to people, "I saw rivets popping out of the wing of my airplane."
- the first one to yell "I see an engine coming off" will be issued a parachute.
- the airline wouldn't let the plane fly if they thought there was any chance of its crashing.
- if you are not generous the first time you order room service, for the remainder of your stay, all the way up with your order, the waiter will have his penis in your soup.
- "No tipping allowed or expected" means no tipping allowed or expected.
- in America, "Have a nice day" means "Have a nice day."
- the elevator inspection card in hotels is actually in the front office for you to see and is actually signed by someone who has something to do with elevators.
- the good-looking, silver-haired couples featured in brochures are actually guests who were caught off guard by a photographer.
- the total you pay for your rental car will match to the penny the total you figured out according to their newspaper ad.
- English-speaking people who know the city streets by heart are not allowed to drive cabs in New York City.
- hotel security guards' main function is to prove that there is employment after death.
- airport insurance companies don't mail the policies to the bene-factors until finding out the plane has landed safely.
- there is a prize to the man who finds an airport bathroom stall that locks.
- women, blacks, Hispanics, and Indians in America don't want to become pilots.
- you can open airline peanut bags without your teeth.
- in spite of indisputable evidence that no plane has ever crashed when all the passengers were nude, the airlines will still not allow nudity on board.
- airport security personnel in the United States all spoke and

understood English, before working too closely to the X-ray machines.

- by requesting it before checking out, you can get a copy of the employee of the month's photograph.
- if you leave shoes in the hall to be shined in an American hotel, in the morning you will have shoes.
- the popularity of the American tourist abroad is on a definite upswing.
- the "ugly American" label was caused by four couples from the South and Midwest who traveled extensively using different aliases.
- there is another train company besides Amtrak.
- Miami Beach telephone weather reports are prerecorded months in advance.
- if you attach an out-of-state license plate on the back of a mad dog, an off-duty Southern highway patrolman will chase it on foot until he catches it or has a coronary.
- there are only 2,349 Japanese tourists in the world, but they travel so much, everyone thinks there are lots more.
- when the Japanese have purchased the United States, they will make Disneyland the nation's capital.
- Japanese businessmen leaving Japan are issued blue suits, white shirts, and blue ties at the Tokyo airport.
- luggage companies really build bags that will last forever or for sixty miles, whichever comes first.
- there is a bill in Congress to make fat people pay more on planes, buses, and trains.
- traveling with your buddies somewhere to shoot a rabbit in the eye or a young deer and his mother in the neck is a sport and a lot of fun.
- when they say there is no waiting at their chair lifts, they mean no waiting.
- Southern California is coming out with a new airline called Air Head.
- Donald Trump is naming his New York to Atlantic City run the Trump Shuffle.
- if animals had guns and fish had hooks and whales had harpoons, there would still be hunters, fishermen, and whalers.

- you really can't miss a really-can't-miss-it.
- there is a scientific and logical reason why bombs are easier to find after a plane is blown apart into seven million pieces than when it is whole and sitting on the runway.
- even if all airlines took the precautions and actions of El Al airline, there would still be terrorist hijackings.
- Air Arabia gives special rates for bar mitzvahs.
- any boss would gladly give their employees a vacation to recover from their vacations.
- married men with three or four children have more fun on vacation than a bunch of single guys.
- just because island hospitals look like out-of-business boutiques and the doctors look like unemployed Good Humor ice cream vendors, there is no reason not to have your operation there.
- most ruins were built since World War II.
- any American ambassador in any foreign nation will put a black-tie affair second to coming to a prison tomb to see an arrested American citizen.
- since President Bush said he would not rest until every American hostage was safely home, he has not slept.

◊   ◊   ◊   **Adoo, Bar, and Reem**

A million and one things can go wrong when traveling, and if you live to a reasonably decent age, you will probably experience most of them. I devised something that helps you get out of a lot of situations unscathed. It is a made-up foreign language. You memorize a group of words that, if spoken often enough, will make your adversary give up out of frustration. You must remember to act innocent, cooperative, and confused.

Three of the words are *adoo, bar,* and *reem.* Let's create a situation to see how they are employed. Let's say you are confronting an airport ticket clerk. You hand him your confirmed ticket with a reserved seat. Everything should go smoothly, so, of course, it doesn't.

CLERK: "I'm sorry, Mr. Green, our computer doesn't show your reservation and first class is booked solid. You'll have to wait for another flight."

YOU: "Reem adooreem."

CLERK: "What?"

YOU: "Baradoo reem adooreem."

CLERK: "Mr. Green, could you speak a little slower and louder? There's a lot of noise here."

YOU: "Reem bar adoo reemadoo adooreem."

CLERK: (*to other clerk*) "Marge, you speak Spanish, right? Okay, will you tell this guy the computer doesn't show . . ."

YOU: "Reem bar adoobar reem reemadoo?"

MARGE: "That's not Spanish."

CLERK: "What the hell is he, some kinda friggin' Buddhist monk?"

YOU: "Barreem adoo."

CLERK: "Barreem adoo, your ass! Here, give me your ticket. Get on the damn plane and go visit all the other reemadoo wackoffs in your family. I'll bump someone who knows what the hell I'm talking about. Here's your boarding pass."

YOU: "Reemadoo! Reemadoo!"

CLERK: "You're welcomeadoo. Next, please. . . . I'm sorry, Mr. Kaufman, but our computer doesn't show . . ."

▼ ▼ ▼ **What's Your Sign?**

Storybook houses and trees for sale ahead

Major horse manure deposit site ahead

Palms read

No waving

No one over age thirty allowed on road

Jimmy Hoffa could be part of this road

Elvis has never been seen here since he died

Don't cross your eyes while driving

◊   ◊   ◊   **Travel Babble**

There is such a thing as travel talk, a special language spoken only by persons who are in some way connected with traveling. What makes this language more difficult than any other in the world is that what is said and what is meant are in no way related. Imagine what it would be like if every expression in your native language meant something entirely different. Well, that'll give you an idea of Travel Babble. To help you learn and master it, I have drawn up a list of some Travel Babble expressions and their real meanings.

What They Say	*Real Meaning*
"**L**adies and gentlemen, this is the pilot. We may be experiencing some slight turbulence."	"**Y**ou are going to be knocked around so badly, the fillings in your mouth will soon belong to the person seated next to you."
"**W**e hope you enjoy your flight."	"**W**e are hung up as hell and wish none of us had to be here."
"**S**o, sit back, relax, and enjoy the flight."	"**G**et ready for the most frightening experience of your life."
"**W**e know you had a choice and thank you for flying with us."	"**W**e know we were the only game in town and we got you by the short ones."
"**W**elcome aboard the Douglas DC-10 . . ."	"**P**repare to die."
"**W**e shall be serving a complimentary snack."	"**W**arn your stomach the unidentifiable is coming down shortly."
"**O**ur friendly flight attendants are Sarah and Bess in first class and Harriet and Myra in coach."	"**P**repare to meet the Bitches of Eastwick."
"**D**id you call, sir? How may I help you?"	"**O**kay, dung face, what the hell do you want?"
"**W**e are fourth in line and should take off shortly."	"**Y**our children will be grown by the time we lift off."
"**W**e are experiencing some rough weather and will fly up to twenty-eight thousand feet to get above it."	"**I**n a few minutes, God will be smashing us with a snow shovel."

What They Say	*Real Meaning*
"We are going to turn off the cabin lights for those passengers who want to rest."	"We hope you've always wanted to die in your sleep."
"I'll be glad to change this for a Coke."	"Figures someone as ugly as you would also be indecisive."
"You have a choice of Beef Medallions à la Rue de Paris or Chicken Kiev."	"Do you want shoe sole covered with pitch or Bird of Chernobyl?"
"There's going to be a slight stopover while we board some new passengers."	"Invest in local real estate, sell for a profit, live off the capital, so you can enjoy your retirement years here."
"If there is anything we can do to make your flight more enjoyable, please do not hesitate to let us know."	"Personally, we really couldn't care less if your head fell through your ass and broke your neck."
"We fly to more cities than any other airline."	"Your luggage can get lost in more cities than with any other airline."
"We should be landing in a few minutes."	"You have enough time to grow corn."
"Will passenger Abdul Hassim please identify himself."	"There's a bomb on board."
"This trip is worth thirty thousand free miles for all you frequent-flier passengers."	"We have boosted the price on everyone's tickets, so you'd better sign up for the free miles, because you're paying for them anyway."
"Would you like a second cup of coffee?"	"Would you like to see if you can drink more dark urine?"

What They Say	*Real Meaning*
"**W**ill the gentleman who ordered the kosher meal please identify himself to a flight attendant."	"**W**e are going to play 'Let's find the Jew.' "
"**T**hat noise you heard is the landing gear being lowered into place for landing."	"**J**esus Christ, what the hell was that?"
"**W**e are about to begin our in-flight movie."	"**W**e hope you want to see this for the third time."
"**B**etween the copilot and myself, we have one hundred and twenty years of flying experience."	"**T**his plane is being piloted by a ninety-seven-year-old man."
"**Y**our bags will be coming out on carousel five."	"**L**eave the airport and take a cab to the nearest clothing store."
"**B**ye. Thank you. Enjoy your day. See you on another flight. Bye now."	"**T**hank God you are getting off, you pigs."
"**L**et me help you with your bags and find you a taxi."	"**I** don't work here, sucker."
"**T**axi?"	"**Y**ou are about to pay more for each mile you travel than it cost to build the highway."
"**W**hat way you want me to take?"	"**L**et me find out if you're a tourist, so I can cheat the hell out of you."
"**T**hat's forty-three dollars and fifty cents including suitcases and highway tax."	"**I** knew you were from out of town the minute I spotted you."
"**H**ave a nice stay."	"**S**o long, sucker."

What They Say	*Real Meaning*
"I don't see your reservation here."	**"A** fifty will do."
"Sorry, there is nothing we can do about it."	**"O**ne hundred dollars will cover it."
"Front."	**"W**e should be able to locate a bellhop in a few hours."
"We'll send your bags up in a few minutes."	**"W**e'll give you an excuse note for your wrinkled suit at your meeting."
"We hope your stay here will be a pleasant one."	**"P**ay in advance, no refunds, not responsible for lost or stolen articles, or injuries leading to permanent disability, loss of limb or life."
"Our highly trained staff offers friendly, courteous service and will bend over backward to accommodate any requests you might have."	**"A**ll our employees are illegal aliens without green cards."
"Of course, you can drink the water."	**"Y**ou will thank your lucky stars we don't charge for toilet paper by the roll."
"Stop worrying. I told you everything is taken care of. The neighbors are going to take in our mail and I turned off the gas."	**"T**he fire department said it looked like the post office blew up."
"Heated pool."	**"T**he water is so cold, you won't even be able to go to the bathroom in it."
"You chose a great time to visit. The weather's been perfect."	**"S**cientists are still baffled by what caused an earthquake of that magnitude."

What They Say	*Real Meaning*
"You can adjust your own air-conditioning and heat."	"I hope you brought medicines for frostbite and jungle fever."
"Your room is being prepared right now."	"This would be a good time to take the grand tour of the city, day and night."
"We'll call you at seven. Have a good night's sleep."	"Make backup reservations on a later flight."
"People rarely use the ice machine after nine P.M."	"You'll be awake all night."
"Delicious local food at reasonable prices."	"Lots of animals cross the highway right here."
"Spicy food? I love spicy food. It doesn't affect me in the slightest."	"I still think two hundred and seventy dollars is a lot of money to replace a toilet."
"Welcome. May I recommend the house wine, which is a blend of the finest sun-drenched, plump, juicy, California valley grapes, aged in wood-treated crocks dating back to the seventeenth century when, as you know, winemaking was an art?"	"We saw you coming and have a pitcher of snake urine for you."
"Even though I never drink, I'm on my vacation and don't think a couple glasses of wine will hurt."	"I don't remember asking for a tattoo of a nuclear sub between my nipples attacking a Russian carrier hiding between my shoulder blades, and I have no idea who shaved my head and put that farm animal in my bed."
"Just try a little piece."	"Congratulations. You have unwittingly eaten your first mongoose nostril."

What They Say	*Real Meaning*
"The chef recommends the Lamb Bouchette à la Roma."	"We've got two potloads of that crap left."
"It is a local recipe eaten for centuries."	"Dog."
"No tipping allowed."	"How would you like me to put my dick in your coffee?"
"Excuse me, I have to go to the bathroom."	"You've got the check, pal."
"Ladies and gentlemen, please welcome local favorites Romero and Angelita Gomez."	"Two people who don't understand one word of Spanish are about to con you into thinking the dance they are about to screw up is an authentic local dance."
"Let's hear it for them."	"Okay, so we conned you, but you can at least be good sports and applaud."
"Come on, you'll love camping. Give it a try."	"One of your children will be carried off by a giant potato bug and will never be seen again. You will be bitten by something for which they have no known antidote. Your Porta Potty will explode—while you're on it. You will join P.A.N.—People Against Nature."
"I know exactly where we are."	"The Western Hemisphere."
"The children will be no problem on the ride there."	"You will try to give yourself a vasectomy with a butter knife."

What They Say	*Real Meaning*
"You can't miss it."	"You will be driving in circles so long, your car will be a classic but you'll be too senile to know what to do about it."
"Anytime you want me to take the wheel, let me know."	"If you even hint at me driving, I'll solder your seat belt closed."
"We're making great time, so far."	"As soon as Triple A gets here, I'll buy a new muffler and we'll be on our way."
"If you take this dirt road here, it should take you back to the main highway."	"In a little while from now, if you see an aircraft overhead, you'd better spell out SOS using your children's clothing and then set your car on fire."
"Isn't it cute how the dog keeps its head out the window of the car and lets the wind blow on her?"	"A car will soon whip by you, causing the most horrendous sight you've ever seen, and your children will be in therapy through their early forties."
"We're here at last."	"Anyone can mistake Washington, DC, for Washington State. At least we're safe."
"American Schamerican. Traveler's checks are traveler's checks."	"Ask them if they'll buy a gold watch."
"Hey, we must vacation together real soon."	"If either you or your demented wife call us to take even a short walk to the corner with you, I'll volunteer you for proctological experiments."

What They Say	*Real Meaning*
"First time here?"	"We are a very boring couple who will bend your ears with nonsense and embarrass you in public to the point where you will cross the Sahara Desert to get away from us, but we'd like to spend your vacation with you anyway."
"Welcome home, Mom and Dad."	"Damn, couldn't you have stayed away a little longer so we could've thrown another party and done it in your bed again?"
"I highly recommend you go there."	"Why should I be the only one to make a mistake?"
"Hi. Whatcha doing?"	"I'm home at last and really need a lot of personal tender love and care. May I come over? Better yet, would you come over here? I never want to leave my house again for the rest of my life!"

◆ ◆ ◆ Common Sen-Sen Sense

The "customer is always right" philosophy went out with bell-bottom pants in America. When I worked all the lousy jobs I had as a boy and young man, I had to take all the lip the customer gave me. Nowadays, even when you are right, you are wrong. No one is going to help you if your hotel room smells like a million cigars died in it, if cold air is blasting down your neck in a restaurant, if your rental car has two flat tires and the doors won't open. Unless . . .

Sen-Sen to the rescue. That's right, those tiny black breath fresheners that taste like spicy licorice. Well, if a few of them are placed in the right place, such as on a restaurant tablecloth or around the table legs, or in a tub or sink, or on the dash of a rental car, the results are immediate and amazing.

"Excuse me, I don't mean to be a bother, but do you think the Health Department could identify if those rat droppings are from a male or female rat?"

"Sorry to make you come all the way up to my room, but I was just wondering if you could figure out how many rats it takes to make a deposit like that?"

"Before I mail this Polaroid picture of the rat droppings on the dash of my rental car to your local newspaper, I thought you might want to look again for a different car for me."

It is said that there's a rat in every crowd. Well, just in case there isn't, create one.

Things You Hate to See

- A flight attendant running to the cockpit.

- A flight attendant coming out of the cockpit crying.

- A flight crew with hands in their pockets, whistling casually, heading for the back of the plane, wearing parachutes.

- Seaweed on the wings of a plane.

- A dead deer tied to the wing of the plane.

- A pilot wearing a cap with a spinning propeller on top of it.

- A pilot and copilot holding hands.

- A pilot grabbing his crotch and telling passengers to "Fly this."

- A pilot giving passengers the finger.

- A pilot mooning passengers and crew.

- A pilot seated in cockpit with his pants down around his ankles.

- A long line at the flight-insurance counter next to your gate.

- Dead bugs on the lenses of your pilot's sunglasses.

- As you enter the plane, the flight crew is repacking oxygen masks.

- Your suitcase coming down the conveyer belt followed by what was packed inside it.

- In baggage claim, your underwear comes out, then your enema bag, then your vibrator, then . . .

- People on the ground running like hell as you are taking off.

- A hole at the bottom of your airsick bag.

- Seeing your suitcase coming off your plane, as your plane is taking off.

- The in-flight movie being fast-forwarded.

- Fabulous view of the Sierras from where the passengers across from you used to be.

- A dead canary in the airplane bathroom.

▶ ▶ ▶ So, What's It Like?

You want to make your greatest vacation even better? All you have to do is call a relative or friend back home.

"... Okay, I'll look at it when I get back. So, what's the weather like? ... That cold? ... Some windchill. ... How many inches? ... Through next weekend? Wow! ... What? ... Eighty-four and sunny!" *Slam!*

It will make you feel sooooooooooooooo goooooooooooood.

▼ ▼ ▼ What's Your Sign?

One shoe on highway up ahead

High airplane crash area

Be on lookout for bald tires

Mother-in-law crossing

Keys almost as big as a car for sale ahead

Flying cups and saucers

Now owned by Japan

People allowed to sit on tires here

▼ ▼ ▼ Help!

When you travel, especially away from your natural environment, there is always the danger of contracting diseases and other physical ailments. Most of them can be prevented or treated, if you are aware of them and know the symptoms. In addition, as in all human endeavors and activities, there are phobias particular to the traveler. I have composed a list of the most common traveler's diseases and phobias.

Hotelstuffitus (Hoe-tel-stuff-eye-tus)
The inability to resist taking everything that isn't nailed down in your hotel room and then stuffing it into your suitcase and taking it home. Long-term sufferers even remove what is bolted down.

Symptoms: You know you have this rather common disease if your home can legally be declared a Ramada Inn; if you feel no guilt when hanging a Sheraton towel on an Arco station towel rack in your bathroom at home; if you wrestle a hotel maid in the hallway for the monogrammed face towel; and when you select a hotel only because their towels match the wallpaper in your guest bathroom.

Cincybizzo (Sin-sea-biz-oh)
This is the fear that on a very long flight, seated next to you will be a businessman from Cincinnati who would never believe that there is a human being alive who wouldn't be fascinated by the long story of his company's merger.

Symptoms: You check to see if the person next to you is wearing white socks; you wear a hearing aid and constantly bang your fist on the dead battery case; as soon as you take your seat on a plane, you begin speaking a language even you don't understand; in the airport bathroom, prior to getting on your flight, you put on a fake Mohawk wig and decals of skulls and crossbones on your arms.

Wishuwerphobia (Wish-you-were-fo-bee-ah)
Paranoia that the person to whom you sent the postcard on which you wrote "Wish you were here" will take it literally and join you on your vacation.

Symptoms: Believing that every fat couple you see is Al and Betty Samarkowski; not mailing postcards until you are back home for at least a month; sending postcards from places you are not visiting; adding a P.S. on card, such as "The doctors still don't know what caused my highly contagious rash that is still bubbling and itching, but the highly contagious diarrhea is now with me only twenty-three hours a day."

Takumwittusitus (Tay-kum-wit-us-eye-tus)
This disease begins to strike just before you and your spouse leave on that much-awaited vacation or second honeymoon, when, all of a sudden, you decide that it would be great to take your children with you.

Symptoms: The main symptom is a total lapse of memory of how the kids absolutely destroyed every moment of happiness on your last vacation; feeling sorry for them, even though they seem to not care less that you are going without them; completely forgetting the meaning of "nervous breakdown."

Wreckarentalitus (Reck-ah-ren-tal-eye-tus)
This is when, knowing the rental car doesn't belong to you, you decide to do all the things you would never do while behind the wheel of your own car.

Symptoms: The first symptom is when, instead of moving up slowly behind car in front of you that is stopped for a red light, you floor the accelerator and slam on the brakes only inches from its rear bumper; the second is when you buy a crash helmet and install a roll bar in your rental car; the third, you swerve to hit cows; and finally, in a car wash, you try to pass the car in front of you.

Passportpicphobia (Pass-port-pic-fo-bee-ah)
This is the psychotic fear that you are beginning to look like your passport photo and that the metamorphosis is inevitable.
Symptoms: You stare at your face in a mirror, close one eye, half close the other eye, pull ten hairs to stand straight up in the air, jam your tongue into your lower lip and open your mouth, and allow saliva to drool out of the corner of your mouth past the ink smudge you put on your cheek, in order to duplicate that once-in-a-lifetime look you had the day you took your passport photo. Other symptoms include believing that the custom guard will look at your passport photo, then at you, then back to the photo, and say, "Perfect"; fear that the immigration inspector is going to stamp your face instead of your passport; that someone will look at your passport seriously, but when they look at you, become hysterical; looking for perforated numbers above your head and your signature across your chest.

Tookusvaporlockus (Took-us-veh-per-lock-us)
This is the phobia that when you sit down on a toilet seat in an airplane, your behind will vapor lock and you will get sucked out over Oklahoma.
Symptoms: You think you see the top of someone's head inside the bowl; before sitting down, you tie a rope around your waist and attach it to the neck of the fattest person on board; you don't raise the lid of the toilet when you go; you make in your purse or attaché; when you go to the rest room, you take with you a map of Oklahoma.

Machoitus (Mah-cho-eye-tus)
This disease strikes men of all ages, although middle is the most common; of all shapes, although out-of is the most common; by making them believe they can do anything physical they want to do or used to be able to do.
Symptoms: Some of the telling signs are verbal, such as statements like "Water skiing? Anyone can water ski!" or "Mountain climbing? What's the big deal?" The physical symptoms include looking in a full-length mirror after showering and really believing you

haven't changed since eleventh grade; thinking that the fact you can swing your feet out of bed in the morning is an indication that you can play tennis for five hours in the island sun; you judge your being in shape by the size of your wrists and ankles.

Upchuckbabephobia (Up-chuck-bay-b-fo-bee-ah)

This is the fear, present during your entire trip, aboard any form of transportation, that the baby seated next to you will throw up on you.

Symptoms: Believing you saw the baby's head spin a full 360°; trying to attach an airsick bag under the breast of the mother; having a rubber dress suit made. Also, you keep waiting for the baby to look at you, wink, and then put its finger down its throat; the buttons on the mother's blouse and skirt look to you to be caked balls of dried Pablum; as soon as someone sits down next to you with a baby in her lap, you shove your finger down your throat to get the baby before the baby gets you.

Bugzapitus (Bug-zap-eye-tus)

This is the fear that, while camping or vacationing in the country, you will sleepwalk naked into an electric bug zapper.

Symptoms: You find yourself running at full speed away from all blue lights; you sleep in asbestos underwear; you cover your privates whenever someone snaps their fingers; you are very nervous at a weenie roast.

Nothingtherephobia (Noth-ing-th-air-fo-bee-ah)

The omnipresent fear that nothing—hotel, rental car, flight, luggage, city, country—will be there when you arrive.

Symptoms: You ask everyone you know and meet if they've been where you are going; you use up all your film in your home before leaving; you don't pack anything; you take only enough money for a movie and a snack; you leave your driver's license and credit cards at home; you don't tell anyone you are going; you leave threats on your travel agent's answering machine.

Greenergrassaphobia (Grr-een-r-grr-ass-ah-fo-bee-ah)
Being convinced, regardless of where you are and how much of a good time you are having, there is a better place to be at that very moment.
Symptoms: Spending most of your vacation perusing brochures from other places; calling friends and asking them to describe where they are and what it's like; calling your travel agent and telling her the joke is over, and she is to get you to "you know where" right away; before leaving home asking your mother-in-law if she is happy about your destination; deciding never to go there again, before you go there for the first time; taking a survey of where the locals who left town on vacation went.

Misstourphobia (Miss-tore-fo-bee-ah)
The fear that you are going to be left behind by your tour bus and wander aimlessly around a foreign country until you are imprisoned for life, pass away, or both.
Symptoms: Never letting go of the sleeve of a fellow passenger; taking Polaroid pictures of bus driver and tour guide and looking at them constantly; continually asking tourists if they recognize you from anywhere; never leaving your tour bus to see anything; never leaving your hotel to get onto the tour bus; never leaving your home to travel to the hotel to get onto the tour bus; applying for a job as a tour-bus driver.

Mixemupitus (Mix-em-up-eye-tus)
This disease is confusing one country with another and having no idea you are doing it.
Symptoms: When you speak the native language, no one understands you; people refuse to accept your money; all the people changed their skin pigmentation; not understanding why they changed all their signs into a foreign language; the most important sight has been torn down and replaced with old buildings; discovering that all the people from this country traded places with the people living in the next country you visit.

Didnotseephobia (Did-knot-sea-fo-bee-ah)
The fear that you didn't see all there is to see or missed one of the most important things to see.
Symptoms: You continually check and recheck every travel guide and map; you look down every street; whispering to locals, "Okay, where is it?"; you follow groups of three or more, including workers breaking for lunch and people heading home; you call everyone you know who has been there and ask what they saw; you decide to never leave the place you're visiting.

Karlmaldenitus (Car-ell-mall-din-eye-tus)
An affliction of the irresistible urge, whenever you hear that someone has lost, misplaced, or forgot their traveler's checks, to yell, "What will you do? What will you do?"
Symptoms: Always wearing a gray hat and a red, bulbous nose; looking for someone to remove their hand from a woman's pocketbook; always listening for the words "Stop, thief!"; staying up late at night worrying how Michael Douglas is doing; waiting for people to walk up and tell you how much they enjoyed watching you on "The Streets of San Francisco."

Oppositphobia (Opp-po-sit-fo-bee-ah)
A strong feeling that in case of an emergency on a plane or heavy turbulence, you will put your head into the airsick bag and throw up between your legs.
Symptoms: Spending an inordinate amount of time checking the size of the airsick-bag opening; squeezing the sides of your head together; putting Preparation H on your hair; greasing yourself from the neck up; staring admiringly at passengers with smaller heads than you; sewing a Hefty Bag between your legs; replacing airsick bag with shopping bag; placing rubber sheet over lap; putting small Mae West inside the front of your underwear; attaching a tiny scuba mask to your private parts; right before takeoff stripping naked from waist down.

Longlostbrophobia (Long-lost-bro-fo-bee-ah)
Paranoia that the foreign bellhop leading you to your room will turn out to be a long-lost brother from the time your father was there during World War II.
Symptoms: Staring at the profile of the bellhop; when the bellhop comments on the weather, replying, "I didn't have a father"; casually mentioning that your father was 106 years old when you were born; overtipping the bellhop, with the words, "It'll be better for everyone if you don't say anything."

Hairoopsphobia (Hare-oop-ss-fo-bee-ah)
Living with the fear that someone is going to compliment your spouse on her change of hair color since they saw the two of you at the last convention or business conference—and you weren't with her the last time.
Symptoms: Before leaving on the trip, you ask your spouse to shave off all her hair, or to color her hair rainbow; you demand your mate wear a hat and never take it off; you walk with your arm around your mate's head; as soon as someone approaches you, you scream, "I was so lonely at our last meeting being alone without my mate, that this time, not like the last time, I brought my spouse along with me, this time, not like the last time, and let's not discuss hair!"; the day of your trip, you ask for a divorce; you quit your job.

Writebookitus (Right-buk-eye-tus)
An incurable disease that strikes after spending most of your life traveling, making you feel that you know enough about the subject to write a book on it.
Symptoms: Making traveling jokes while sailing, and having child-hood friends agree it would be funny in a book; telling travel stories and ideas to friends to get their reactions; talking a publisher into doing the book; spending months jotting down ideas on three-by-five cards; buying an expensive word processor; taking hours of word processor instructions; practicing for hour after hour on word processor, the result of which is occasionally

being able to delete a word; giving away word processor after two months and digging out the old manual typewriter; spending months working around the clock typing and retyping book; finally finishing the book and swearing on all you hold sacred that you'll never write another book; going to Caribbean island to sit on the beach and do nothing, then getting another great idea for a book . . .

▲ ▲ ▲ **Love It or Leave It**

People throughout the world have great nationalistic and civic pride. For some inexplicable reason, the fact that our parents happened to be in this place instead of that place when we slipped out or were extracted makes us believe, wholeheartedly and eternally, that our house, our street, our neighborhood, our section of our city, our city in our state in our region of our country in our hemisphere, is far superior to anyone else's, in spite of the fact that others feel exactly the same about their own location. There is no way anyone could ever convince me that the greatest place in the whole world isn't 1431 South Fourth Street, in South Philadelphia, Pennsylvania, United States of America, Western Hemisphere, worth fighting and even dying for, unless, of course, they were to show me proof that I was actually born in a house at 1431 Xerxes Street in Minneapolis, Minnesota.

By taking advantage of this pride, you can get almost anything accomplished, corrected, or avoided. The following will show you how to use this weapon to your own advantage and comfort.

—"I just can't believe Denver would have such rough toilet paper."

—"Who would've ever imagined that hotel rooms were so small in Arizona?"

—"I thought the people back home were joking when they told me that Austrians were so money hungry."

—"Who said that British cabbies are the friendliest in the world?"

—"How come some people think the Danes are so generous? I haven't seen it yet!"

—"Treated like a brother in Japan? What a joke."

—"I've yet to see what's changed in Russia."

—"Never in my wildest dreams did I ever imagine a German taking advantage of another human being." (Well, maybe this is stretching it.)

Now, I'll give you an actual incident that happened to me which I think best demonstrates taking advantage of civic pride. My friend and I were in Rome for only one day and night, before returning to the States. I had been there on several occasions, but this was her first visit and she had always wanted to see the ruins. We got to them just as they were closing. Telling her to flash her great smile did nothing to change the minds of the guards. I went for the second-greatest mover in the world. I offered them money, lots of it. Nothing. I told them it was her birthday. Zero. Our only day in town. Deaf ears. It was my last year to live. Zip. I said my real name was Brennero. Getting warm. Then I hit them with the big gun.

"If it weren't for that piece-of-crap airline, Alitalia, getting us here so late, we would've made it in plenty of time. Never again. We'll fly Swissair home. Ciao."

Not only did they let us in, but they told us to take all the time we wanted. The ruins were great, but not nearly as good as the ones in my old neighborhood in Philadelphia.

◇ ◇ ◇ **The Car,
James**

This is not an original idea; I learned it from
a friend who pulled it off successfully for years. It is for that time in
life when your ego and spirit could use some soft, kid-glove
handling and you're able to lock your conscience in your suitcase.

When you come out of any half-decent hotel, there is usually a
line of limousines waiting to pick up their clients. It is customary
for drivers to hang together shooting the breeze. You walk up to
within five feet of the group, cross your arms in front of your chest,
plant a scowl on your face, and say, "Well?" Immediately, one of
the drivers will inquire if you are his customer.

"Mr. Parsnappier?"

"Let's get going, if you don't mind," you snap.

"Right away, sir. Here, let me get the door for you."

"Thank you. I'm in a bit of a hurry."

"I'll have you at the Starling Restaurant in ten minutes, Mr.
Parsnappier."

"I'm going to the airport. My brother is the one going to the
restaurant. After you drop me off, come back for him. Watch out,
too. He's a bit eccentric and absentminded. Matter of fact, he often
denies that I even exist, so don't even mention that you saw me."

"Yes, Mr. Parsnappier."

Give the driver a big tip. After all, that's all it costs you.

I have a feeling your experiences in the backseat of a stretch
limo will begin with your next trip. I only hope you don't take mine.

◆ ◆ ◆ Help Is Only a Fingertip Away

The following is probably the most important travel information of all, and yet, it is virtually unknown even to the most experienced traveler. There is a phone number you can dial for an immediate answer to almost every question, or to get help for almost any situation.

You can now roam anyplace in the world, regardless of how remote or dangerous, knowing that help is only a fingertip away. The prefix is always 1-500-555 followed by the four numbers listed below. So, for example, in order to reach "southern Yugoslavian bird calls," you would dial 1-500-555-0001. I suggest you carry a reduced xerox copy of this list with you whenever you travel.

0002—Northern Yugoslavian bird calls.

0003—Closest 7-Eleven store.

0004—Farthest 7-Eleven store.

0005—Story of birth of 7-Eleven stores narrated by Mahatma Gandhi.

0006—Italy's latest government officials updated hourly.

0007—Someone else bitching vehemently about a lost suitcase.

0008—Local sexual diseases and where to get them.

0009—Spouse complaining so you don't get homesick.

0010—Excuses for not having sex so you don't miss your spouse at night.

0011—For men, a female voice saying all the things you've never heard said, including the classic "I hate to shop."

0012—For women, a male voice saying all the things you've never heard said, including the classic "I'm falling in love with your mind."

0013—Local Bo Diddley look-alikes.

0014—Exxon daily oil spill update.

0015—Hair transplant reweaving.

0016—Famous Quaker Ninjas.

0017—Record a message for your boss that will never be delivered.

0018—Five places to go within thirty-seven seconds.

0019—A reminder to take your pills.

0020—What your mate is doing at that exact moment.

0021—Local divorce laws.

0022—Sounds of someone eating a Big Mac and an apple pie à la mode.

0023—Pat Nixon and Nancy Reagan talking dirty.

0024—Local Jehovah's Witness bowling league.

0025—Native way of saying "Up yours, pig face!"

0026—Tips on what gets local women hot.

0027—Believable excuses for anything.

0028—The meaning of life and how to get a broken key out of a car door.

0029—Chinese names that rhyme with Ping, Pong, and Stein.

0030—The latest sighting of Elvis.

0031—Cow-dip-throwing final scores and update.

0032—What was really in that meal you just ate.

0033—Pep talk to convince you not to call home.

0034—1,001 excuses for not calling home.

0035—Reasons you can give why your trip is terrible, just in case you do call home.

0036—A voice from your past.

0037—Laugh track from President Bush's speeches.

0038—Latest monologues of Johnny Carson, David Letterman, Arsenio Hall, and Dan Quayle.

0039—How to rest during periods of political unrest.

0040—Where your ambassador ran when it hit the fan.

0041—Other tourists who are lost and in a panic.

0042—Boring countrymen who are in the area.

0043—Better things you could've done with your money.

0044—The odds of getting home.

0045—Newly discovered neuroses by Richard Lewis

0046—Steve Landesberg doing impression of local police chief.

0047—Heavy local breathing.

0048—A description of *Penthouse*'s present centerfold.

0049—Eddie Murphy laughing.

0050—Places where the weather is currently better.

0051—Things to do alone in your hotel room when it rains.

0052—The local emergency phone number when the other one didn't answer.

0053—The most recent purchase of property in America by a Japanese.

0054—A Rumanian folk song dealing with scarves.

0055—Last year's winning lottery numbers.

0056—Places giving the worst haircuts in the world.

0057—How to develop a new laugh.

0058—Toilet paper substitutes.

0059—What that smell is.

0060—For drunks who are too drunk to dial the number they really want to call.

0061—Lies about how great your stocks are doing so you can enjoy your trip.

0062—Which ruins are fake.

0063—Which fakirs are ruined.

0064—Odds on your mate sleeping alone while you're away.

0065—Name of person with whom your mate is sleeping while you're away.

0066—How to best remove sheep blood from car bumpers.

0067—Where you went wrong in life.

0068—What to do when poisoned with only thirty minutes to live and the phone number of person who will do it with you.

0069—Secret word of the day.

0070—First and second names of the lesser gods.

0071—Things people at home are saying about you.

0072—Fun things to do with a piece of string, beeswax, a horn, and a duck.

0073—Popular local daydreams.

0074—Last year's train schedule.

0075—Caring for a hernia until you can get medical attention.

0076—Latest soccer deaths.

0077—Who Sugar Ray Leonard is going to fight in the year 2014.

0078—Places you could've left your wallet.

0079—Karl Malden's home phone number.

◇ ◇ ◇ # The World's Lightest Luggage

I planned a fantastic five-week vacation. Two weeks sailing the Caribbean aboard a 138-foot schooner built in 1938, one week in Rio, and then the Concorde from Caracas to Tel Aviv for the last two weeks.

One problem. A major one. All the differences in environments, activities, and weather would require major baggage. If anything can put a monsoon damper on a good time, it's packing, unpacking, packing, unpacking, checking, carrying, and worrying about a lot of baggage. I figured out a simple solution.

I took only clothes I no longer wanted to wear, things I was about to give to charities anyway. As each phase of the trip ended, I would leave the clothes for whoever was there: the sailboat crew, the housekeepers in Rio. By the time I got to Israel, I had only one bag and a topcoat. When I left Israel, I had only a toiletry kit containing a toothbrush, toothpaste, shaver, after-shave, traveler's checks, and my passport. I walked into the airport in Tel Aviv with the lightest luggage in the world and into one of the heaviest problems I had ever encountered while traveling.

The Israeli security guard looked at my little shaving kit and then at me. She studied my face. I smiled. She didn't.

"Where is the rest of your luggage?"

"There isn't any. This is it."

I couldn't wait for her to ask me why that's all I had, so I could explain my brilliant plan.

"How long have you been traveling?"

This was getting good.

"Five weeks. Five *long* weeks."

Come on, ask, already.

"Where have you been traveling?"

Wait'll she hears this one.

"I sailed the Caribbean, spent a week in Rio, stopped in Paris, and then came here."

She's got to ask now.

"All those countries for all that time and all you have is this little bag?"

B-I-N-G-O!

I almost leapt into the air, clicked my heels, and let out a squeal like a TV game-show host, but a thought suddenly came to mind. Israel is a very poor nation because 90 percent of its income-tax dollars go for national defense to prevent the Arab nations from carrying out their threat of pushing them into the sea. How would they ever believe a story about giving away clothes? I remember when I was poor and found something in a trash can, like a vest or a glove, I couldn't believe someone threw it away. I was in a lot of trouble.

"Eh . . . you see . . . I . . . [great start, David] . . . I left everything with my girlfriend at the Hilton Hotel."

It was a partial truth. The only falsehood was that I left only my Israel clothes. If they went there, they would never believe that I stood on the deck of a sailboat wearing a suit and overcoat. I had one trump card. My girlfriend was the most popular singer in Israel! I mentioned her name.

"You know who she is, right?"

"Everyone in Israel knows who she is. She is marvelous."

I smiled. She signaled for the two Israeli security guards with the cold eyes and Uzis. They were very thorough in their examination. Let me put it this way, they found out what I had eaten for the past two days. After an hour in that small, hot examining room, I was escorted through security check and told to sit with other passengers who were taking my El Al flight to New York.

My paranoia was inflamed. I convinced myself that they were just letting me sit here to raise my confidence level. Then right before they began boarding, the guards would return and escort me out for interrogation. Even though I was innocent of any wrongdoing, I—a Jew whose father's family were Palestinians from way back when, the grandson of a prominent rabbi, and a Zionist—did not want to be detained in an Israeli prison.

I was so caught up in my paranoid thoughts that I didn't hear the TWA flight attendant until her third hello. Great. Just what I need—a fan. Wait; this might be my chance.

"Listen, you could help me out of a real jam. I'm going to trust you with an awful truth about me. See that fat woman stuck in that seat over there? Well, I was once engaged to her daughter and chickened out two weeks before the wedding. The mother was livid. You can imagine how much it cost for the eighty-four yards of Indian silk for her wedding tent. The dressmaker got a rupture lifting the veil. Anyway, I can't believe my bad luck. Not only are we on the same flight, but she's sitting next to me, and I know, as soon as I doze off, she's going to put her arm flap over my face and smother me. Can you get me on your flight?"

"It's too late to buy a ticket. We're taking off in a couple minutes."

"Damn."

"But"—she smiled, putting her arm through mine as if we were old friends—"my fiancé is the pilot, so I can just walk you on. Where are your bags?"

"Here."

"You're kidding. Is that all?"

"Please, my ass still hurts from the last people who didn't believe me. I'll tell you the whole story after we're in the air."

When I went through customs in New York, no one questioned my luggage. Figures, right? And I had a great story all ready about not reading the washing instructions on my clothing labels.

More Things You'll Never Hear

- We've perfected the public address system in this train station so it no longer sounds like someone yelling into a toilet ten miles from here.
- Since we don't have a room left, we'll put you into a suite for the price of a room.
- Let us show you a bunch of rooms and you select the one you like best.

- We'll get the people who are occupying your room past the check-out time to vacate it immediately.
- If your room isn't clean enough, please let me know and I'll come right back and redo it.
- Concierge, could you send up a bandage? I was taking a shower and one of your huge bars of soap fell on my foot.
- You can stay as much past the checkout time as you wish, and of course, there will be no extra charge.
- Is that room service already?
- Our food is not too good. Eat in the hotel across the street.
- I had to practically break the maître d's arm before he would accept the tip.
- Let me do it. I love changing tires.
- You can double-park here for as long as you need.
- Yes, I must've scratched it when parking it, so here is a check to have it fixed.
- Although this is a smoking section, if it bothers you, I'll be glad not to smoke during this entire six-hour trip.
- That is such a pleasant-sounding alarm clock.
- If the resort isn't exactly as we described, this agency will pay for your whole trip.
- Anyone can lose a ticket. Forget it.
- Congratulations. You are our one-millionth customer, so . . .
- God loves you. Here, take some money.
- You'll love our water, señor.
- It's *magnifique* having you Americans here.
- Thank you, darling, but I can carry my own bag.
- You are one hundred percent right.
- Please forgive us.
- I'd love to.
- Of course.
- Right away.
- My mistake.
- Anything you want.
- It's free.
- Let me do it.
- I appreciate it.
- Thank you so very, very much.
- Yes, I'll be glad to do that to myself.

GETTING THERE

★ ★ ★ A Flying Vacillation

As always, I arrived at the airport early. I hate rushing for anything. I know I'm there, the plane's there, my bags are probably checked in time to make it onto my flight, my seat is reserved and confirmed, so I can relax enough to start to build up my fear of flying without rushing it.

This time, I arrived at the airport exceptionally early. Matter of fact, they informed me that I could take an earlier flight home.

"Great. I'll take it."

Wait a minute, suppose this earlier plane goes down? A plane I'm not even supposed to be on.

"Hold on. I'll stay with my original flight. I'm in no hurry to get home. Thanks anyway."

Wait a minute. Suppose my scheduled flight goes down and I had an opportunity to change, to live, to be home an hour earlier? Better change it.

"Let's do it. I'll take the earlier flight after all. I just thought of something I could do that first hour home. Thanks."

I may have just thanked someone for helping me sign my death warrant. Better stick to the original and not play with fate. Cancel the change.

"Cancel the change. Sorry. I'll take the original flight. Thanks. Sorry."

Not as sorry as when this plane is nose-diving into a farm somewhere and the earlier flight is already in New York boarding people to come back here who will be looking at the scorched remains of . . . better go earlier.

"Better go earlier. I mean, after all, I'm already here and there's nothing . . . What? . . . Too late? Okay, I'll take my original flight. Sorry to have bothered you."

Do I have to tell you how many times I inquired if the first flight made it safely? Do I have to tell you when I found out that it did, how many times I kicked myself for not taking it? Do I have to tell you how scared and crazed I was from the moment I stepped onto my flight until it landed safely? Do I have to tell you that I still show up at airports early but *never* early enough to take an earlier flight? Do I have to tell you how nuts I am?

▼ ▼ ▼ # What's Your Sign?

Check for bad breath

Keys almost as big as a bed for sale ahead

Large hanging breasts up ahead

 Ks for sale up ahead

 No M-turns allowed

 Make U-turn—immediately!

 Too late

 Light at the end of the tunnel

◆ ◆ ◆ Tick Tock, Tick Tock

In 1988, I sailed across the Pacific aboard the *QE II*, performing shows and joining my father on his fifth cruise around the world. For six days, we had a fantastic time, but I saw nothing but ocean. Because of another commitment, I had to take a flight back to the States the night we arrived in Tahiti. Excluding a farewell dinner with my father, this left me only eight hours' spare time. As wonderful as the trip had been, it would be terrible to be in that part of the world and not see anything. I made a plan and executed it.

A van met me at the dock and took me on a tour of Tahiti. Then I was driven to the airport where I had a small, private plane fly me to the airstrip off Bora-Bora where a speedboat took me across the bay to the island. The waiting taxi sped me to the best beach, where I sunned and swam for a couple hours, before returning to the speedboat, which drove me back to the plane, which flew me to the island of Mooréa, where another taxi took me to another best beach for more sun and surf and a fresh-fish lunch in a beachside restaurant. Into the taxi, into the plane, into a taxi, into my shower aboard the *QE II* and dinner with my father after which another taxi took me to the airport where a jumbo jet flew me to New York via Los Angeles. (I didn't arrange the latter.)

You can't beat the clock, but I don't think you should live by it, either. I believe you should give time one helluva run for its money.

▶ ▶ ▶ # You Name It, I Got It

I believe that I am one of the best-prepared travelers in the world. I don't overpack and I am prepared for just about everything that could transpire, except Godzilla's ripping down the wall of my hotel room or King Kong's picking up my car and eating it.

Let's just take for example my one-month combined trips to Egypt and Kenya in December of 1988, which included a few days in Cairo, a boat trip down the Nile, a couple days in Nairobi, and ten days of living in a tent and going on daily safaris. Cities, deserts, land, water, the bush, ruins, hotels, tents, small planes, hot-air balloons, cars, Land-Rovers, boats, heat, cold, wind, rain, insects, animals, and illnesses. Quite a challenge for even one of the best preparation experts.

Whenever a certain person accompanies me on one of my trips, I am the butt of her jokes because of my fetish for details and preparedness. To avoid her being embarrassed by the following account, let's call her "Ebs." Okay, we are going to Egypt and Kenya, so several weeks before we are to leave, Ebs, in the company of my lifelong friends, performs a spontaneous stand-up routine, highly exaggerated, based on a reenactment of what she classifies as "harassment," which consisted of my telling, or rather, strongly recommending, what she should take on the trip. She regaled everyone. I admit she was extremely funny, although I managed not to laugh, but I felt her performance misrepresented my good intentions and the importance of the subject.

Everyone turned to me at the end of her show for my rebuttal, but I said nothing. If she didn't want to listen to my suggestions, that was her prerogative. For the next few weeks, I said nothing about packing and never again brought up my request of having "the first right of disapproval" of what she was planning to bring with her. I think it was this request, and my objecting to her bringing a hair drier, that caused her adamant rebellion in the first place.

   Needless to say, when it was time to leave for our trip, I had one separate, small bag for Egypt and one separate, small bag for Kenya, and Ebs had one combination, large bag for Egypt and one combination, large bag for Kenya. Needless to say, when we arrived in Cairo, I put away my Kenya bag and unpacked only the top of my Egypt bag. Ebs totally unpacked both of her bags. Needless to say, I was very comfortable walking around in the cold Cairo air in my army fatigue jacket with the lightweight army-issue thermal vest under it. Ebs was shivering in her light jeans jacket. Ebs's imitation of me calling international weather every three or four days before we left on the trip was one of the hysterical highlights of her performance. Matter of fact, my friends actually applauded how she told me to stop bugging her with weather reports. I did stop, and now she was freezing.

   I'm not going to bore you with a list of all the items during that trip that Ebs did not have and I did. I mean, why go into detail about shopping for warm sweaters in Abu Simbel, and how the ones she finally bought smelled like they were sheared off the ass of a two-hundred-year-old sheep? Why describe Ebs running around borrowing turtlenecks from fellow passengers aboard our boat? Let's skip these and similar stories. Let it suffice to speak of three items as representative of all.

   Maalox: You can imagine what a ball Ebs had with this "grandfather's remedy," as she called it. The boat personnel traced the virus to the air-conditioning, but luckily, I don't like to breathe manufactured cold air or heat, so I only use them to take the chill or heat out of my room prior to retiring. Only Ebs and I were not stricken. The passengers who had screamed at Ebs's account of my Maalox—oh, I forgot to mention that she did her whole stand-up for our newfound friends aboard the boat—anyway, these same people sheepishly asked for some of my Maalox. Luckily, it fell into the category of "Necessary Extras," along with a duplicate cap for my eyetooth and a third pair of sunglasses, so I handed it out generously.

   Ebs struggled against the virus for as long as she could, but although not as deadly ill as the others, she finally lost the battle. Her face matched the green of her eyes. I waited; she had to come to me. She did.

"David . . . could you . . . would you . . . I am . . . my stomach . . . please, I . . . oh, hell, I need Maalox."

"Maalox? You want Maalox? The grandpapa's remedy? Ebs, I don't care if you vomit your nostrils. Cramp City is where you're living, babe."

Oh, revenge is so sweet. It makes a turnip taste like sugar. Of course, I gave Ebs all the Maalox she needed. It is especially good after someone eats crow.

Unessentials: I consider myself an expert when it comes to distinguishing between what seems to be unnecessary and isn't and that which appears to be necessary but truly isn't. I award myself such a status because on any given trip I always, always, mind you, use everything. Before going on to Kenya from Egypt, for example, I had already used my magnifying glass, small scissors, penknife, can opener, and flask. You can imagine my horror and disbelief on our last day in Egypt that there was one item I brought with me that remained unused.

Time was running out. We were looking at the last ruin. In a few minutes, we would be returning to the boat for our last night aboard. I must admit, I started worrying. As we stood there looking at another wonder, a fellow passenger, Chuck, turned to his wife, Pat, and asked, "Which direction does that tomb entrance face?"

"What did you say, Chuck?" I inquired excitedly.

"Oh, I was just asking Pat which direction the tomb entrance faces, because I've noticed . . ."

I couldn't care less why he asked the question. I only cared that he had asked it. I fumbled with nervous fingers through one of the eighteen pockets of my hunting vest.

"Which direction? you ask. Well, let me see."

I popped the lid of my miniature compass.

"North by northeast."

"Thanks, David."

"No, thank *you*, Chuck."

I glared at Ebs. Her "small, stupid General George Patton compass" comedy routine still rang in my ears. Without taking my eyes off her, I snapped the lid closed and flipped it into the air, and without looking, I felt it land in one of my pockets. My extra flashlight filter pocket, to be exact.

Raincoats: "David even bought each of us one of those fold-up raincoats you see in old World War Two movies. He says they're for Kenya. It never rains there in January. I'm waiting to get my fold-up snow shovel."

Ebs wasn't entirely accurate. The January rainfall in Kenya isn't zero, it's two-tenths of an inch. However, I always prepare for the unexpected. As a baby, I had an emergency hand brake installed in my stroller—with a backup, of course.

About twenty-five feet from the entrance of our tent in the Masai Mara Reserve in Kenya there was a dried-up riverbed. It was, after all, the dry season. We were told not to expect to see any crocodiles, because their water holes were few and far between, because it was the dry season in Kenya, remember?

As we lay in our tent one night, I heard what I thought were berries falling on top of and bouncing off our tent. Sporadic at first, and then fierce. It was the beginning of what turned out to be a week-long, record-breaking rain spell.

The next morning, at what would've been sunrise, had it not been pouring, I handed Ebs her WWII raincoat, which she silently put on. We got into our Land-Rover and spent a good part of the morning watching and photographing crocodiles.

I have to add two postscripts to this tale.

P.S. At the end of the month away from home, when we were getting dressed to take a cab to the Nairobi airport, I reached into my one, separate Kenya bag, pulled out a small plastic bag, and put on never-been-worn underwear, socks, shirt, and pants. Ebs stood there looking as if all the animals we had seen on safari had stampeded over her. I didn't say anything to her. I didn't have to.

P.P.S. After the Egypt and Kenya experience, Ebs has voluntarily suggested that for any future trips we take together, I can pick out *everything* for her to take. I said I would think about it.

Victory appears in strange and wonderful ways.

More Things You Hate to See

- A dead moose on your fender when you haven't been hunting.

- Face of an FBI Most Wanted on the Good Samaritan who picked you up just now when you ran out of gas.

- Your youngest child in your rearview mirror as you pull out of a gasoline station.

- Crumpled police evidence tag in the trunk of the used car you just purchased.

- No bits and pieces of car engine on road in front of you but lots of them on road behind you.

- A semi directly in front of you, a semi directly behind you, and a semi passing you, as you are going up a steep hill of a dirt road during a torrential downpour.

- Your spouse's pet parakeet when you turn on your windshield wipers to high speed.

- The paper bag no longer over your parking meter.

- A racing stripe on your car that wasn't there when you gave it to the parking attendant.

- No one you recognize on your tour bus.

- On the dash of the tour bus a statue of Jesus wearing a baseball cap.

- A sign on the dashboard of your bus reading I DON'T BRAKE FOR DOGS, SALESMEN, FAGS, JEWS, SPICS, OR NIGGERS.

- Across the front exterior of the bus are indented impressions of the previously mentioned.

- Chicken feathers in the bus.

- Through the window of the train you are on, as it pulls out of the station, you see in the train next to you, going in the opposite direction, your spouse and family in a very similar-looking compartment.

▼ ▼ ▼ Up, Up, and Not Away

The clerk said the flight from San Juan to Antigua was overbooked, so they were putting me on one of these small island planes that are responsible for the death of more fish than all the fishermen in the Caribbean put together. He added that there was absolutely no way anything could be done about it. You know the airline story: "We screwed you. Sorry. Next." I asked the clerk to lean closer and whispered to him.

"Look, I don't want to say this too loudly and scare all the other passengers you have flying on your small plane, but I was on that small one of yours that went down recently, killing all but a couple of us. [Not true, of course, but probable.] So, you can understand my trepidation about getting on one of your [raise voice a little] miniature death traps [lower volume], and I understand how you would hate this to be advertised, especially at this hectic time."

"Let me see what I can do, Mr. Brenner."

"Thanks."

A couple of minutes later, the clerk informed me that I was rebooked on my original flight. He did it by giving a passenger a fifty-dollar rebate to switch planes. I thanked him and started to walk away. He called me back.

"I'm sorry, Mr. Brenner, but you'll have to check your bag. It's too big to carry on."

"I just arrived on your New York flight with it under my seat [true], and besides, the last bag I checked with you people is still circling the globe somewhere [not true, but probable], which really doesn't matter because I wouldn't know what to do with bell-bottom pants now anyway."

He laughed. I carried on the bag.

Final score: Passenger, 2; Airline, 0.

Big upset!

▲ ▲ ▲ Foreign Foolery

Did you ever notice that when some Americans talk to people who have a foreign accent, they act as if the person is deaf and therefore yell at the top of their lungs? Then, adding insult to injury, they talk slowly, as though the person is also an idiot? I've noticed it a lot, because I am one of the idiots who does it. If someone with an accent asks me something, such as "Could you please direct me to the Empire State Building?" I scream at them, "Go bus! Off Thirty-fourth Street! See building big like buffalo!" Thank goodness, I stop a few beats short of doing a rain dance.

◊ ◊ ◊ Don't Look, Don't Talk

"How did you get into show business?"
"Were you always funny?"
"Do you write all your own jokes?"
"What is Johnny Carson really like?"
"Who makes you laugh?"
"Did you hear the one about . . . ?"
These are the most often asked questions of me. People mean well and don't realize how many times I've been asked these same questions. It is especially bad when you are trapped next to someone on a plane. Usually my manager flies with me, but sometimes I'm alone and the flight is crowded. Such was the case once, returning to New York from Los Angeles.

As I boarded the plane, out of the corner of my eye, I saw a stranger already occupying the seat next to mine. Without making eye contact, I slid into my seat, quickly pulled out a bunch of magazines, and buried my face in one. With my peripheral vision, I could see the man next to me was reading a thick book. Great.

When the flight attendant asked what we wanted to drink, we both ordered club sodas with lemon. He had a European accent. Great. He probably had no idea who I am, anyway. But to play it safe, I kept reading. So did he.

When each of us went to the bathroom and returned, we didn't look at each other, and so it went for three peaceful hours. Then the man next to me leaned toward me and whispered, "Don't I know you from somewhere?"

I couldn't believe it. My luck, he does watch TV. My rotten luck. Well, what are you going to do? At least, I got through half the trip. I turned to face him.

"Possibly. My name is . . ."

I was looking into one of my favorite faces. A face that had shared the stage and many TV shows with me. A terrific person. Victor Borge.

We laughed hysterically over how we were both avoiding the stranger in the next seat. The book and magazines were put away, and for the next three hours, we had the most delightful time talking. We covered a lot of interesting subjects, but my favorites were responses to my questions about how he got started in show business, if he was always funny, if he wrote all his own jokes and music, what he thought Johnny Carson was really like, and who made him laugh. I also told him some of my favorite jokes.

It was a great conversation, but for some reason, I haven't heard from Victor since then. Maybe I'll run into him on another flight.

★ ★ ★ # The Lord Has Landed

The last thing I want to see when I get off a plane is someone hustling me for money under the guise of God's name. Imagine some pimpled face, either terribly underweight or overweight, either male or female (for it's hard to tell someone's sex when they have seven hairs on their head and a baggy sheet over their body), trying to tell me they have the answer to life. I'm sure I don't have even the slightest key to any particular aspect of life, but I am certain that one of the answers to life is *not* to look and dress that way and *not* to be a giant pain to people, especially when they are rushing to catch a plane or to get as far away from one as possible.

Whenever one of those religious blights approaches me, I get them first. Just as they are about to whine their spiritual message, I point my finger at them, and in my most authoritative voice, I say, "God was on my plane. He wants to talk to you!"

It stuns them long enough for me to make my escape. Thank God.

◆ ◆ ◆ # A Different Perspective

My travel agent and my personal manager know my two unbreakable rules of travel: (1) no DC-10's, and (2) no small planes. Ever!

After a gig at an upstate New York university, we headed for our plane at the airport. I stopped. The plane looked like a painted shoe box with model plane wings on it. Like some demented kid had built it for a school project.

"This is a joke, right, Steve?"

"It was the only flight."

"Let's drive."

"It's six hours to New York and it's supposed to rain, and—"

"If it rains hard enough, it'll help put out the fire after that thing crashes. Rent a car."

"They're boarding."

"Get their names. I'll send their families condolence cards."

"David, you're going to have to get over your fear of small planes sometime."

"Fly my casket to the cemetery in one."

"Do you want to live with this fear all your life?"

"Better than not having it and dying in one of those. I'll take a night course in overcoming my fear of dying in planes like that after we don't take a plane like that. Rent a car."

Steve left and returned within five minutes.

"All they have is a station wagon whose brakes are shot. They won't allow us to buy insurance for it. And it's raining hard. The truth. Your call."

As soon as I had to get into a Quasimodo crouch to walk to my seat, I knew I'd made a big mistake. There were strands of hair hanging from the ceiling of the plane that had rubbed off from people walking down the aisle. The pilot was wearing a checkered sport jacket and baseball cap. I swear. When I saw the foam dice hanging on the mirror in the cockpit, I knew I'd made a fatal mistake in deciding to fly, and I mean *fatal.*

On the takeoff, it was like we were in a game of "plane ball," and a giant kicked us off. The noise was horrific and the shaking and vibrating were horrendous. With all the flying I do, I can tell when something is wrong. Something was very, very wrong.

We dropped hundreds of feet, recovered momentarily, then dropped a thousand or more feet. The pilot fought the controls. He was trying to return to the airport. As we headed back, the plane kept dropping and rising. Miraculously, we landed. As soon as the tires touched down, I looked at Steve's ashen face.

"Get the station wagon or two horses."

As I was waiting for Steve, our flight crew and an airline mechanic came out of a room. They saw me. The mechanic held some kind of metal object. Across the crowded airport, he called to me.

"Hey, Dave, the problem was only this forty-nine-cent landing-gear bolt. We put in a new one. Come on. We're going to board."

"Let me tell you something," I called back. "You get a whole new perspective on flying when you see your private parts fly up past your head."

▶ ▶ ▶ **Say What?**

There are many excellent foreign-language translation guides that provide the traveler with the most important and frequently used expressions and key words. However, not one I have seen takes it that extra step, beyond the cutting edge, so to speak. You can only get so far in a foreign country with "Where is the post office?" "Where can I send a telegram?" "Is your uncle coming to dinner?" "Please don't use any oil." "What time do you have?" "Where do they sell trousers?"

Imagine if the vocabulary in your native language consisted only of that found in a traveler's translation dictionary. For example, you are checking into a hotel in Portland, Oregon, and the clerk doesn't have your reservation and the best you can do is to say, "Please be considerate. Do you sell hats?" instead of, "I've got a twelve-pound, ex–Golden Glove fist that says you overlooked my name, you dork!"

I am now going to provide you with the *real* most vital expressions you will need when traveling. All you have to do is either ask your local high school language teacher or student to translate them for you. You are on your way to not being a speechless fish out of water, or more accurately, to not being a schmuck away from home.

First, I'll give you a typical traveling situation and the sequential words you would need to say as translated in several languages. Then comes the categorical listing of expressions for you to translate into the language of your choice.

ENGLISH:	**Excuse me, could you please help me? My suitcase isn't here. Thank you.**
SPANISH:	¿Excuse me, es possible assiste meo? Mi bolsa malet no aqui. Graçias.
FRENCH:	Pardon moi, possible assistez moi? Bagages non arrive. Merci.
ITALIAN:	Scusa, assisto meo? Mi bagali no arriv. Grazie.
GERMAN:	Achtung! Gilsh machen assistant? Meine kasig suitgeben nein komen. Danke.
SWAHILI:	Samahani. Tafadhali, unaweza kunisaidia? Shanta kimepotea. Asante.

ENGLISH:	**My suitcase still isn't here. How about helping me, pal? Okay?**
SPANISH:	Mi bolsa malet stillo no aqui. Assiste meo, amigo? Jo kay?
FRENCH:	Bagages stillez non arrive. Assistez moi, mon ami? Oh kaye?
ITALIAN:	Mi bagali stilo no arriv. Assisto meo, gumba? O-kay?
GERMAN:	Achtung! Meine kasig suitgeben schtill nein komen? Machen assistant, Mein Herr? Oo kach?
SWAHILI:	Shanta kimepotea staeili. Unaweza kunisaidia, bazuri? Okawa?

ENGLISH:	**Listen, mister! It's been two hours! Get my bag!**
SPANISH:	Españada, señor! Este dos horas! Gigame bolsa malet!

FRENCH: Pardonnez, monsieur! C'est deux heurre! Grabon mon bagages!
ITALIAN: Menegro, senore! Esto due horas! Getdado me bagali!
GERMAN: Achtung, Herren! Ich bin zwei heühr. Getenzi mein suitgeben!
SWAHILI: Shanta, bwana! Esbilliji mbill saa. Gesteili shanta kimepotea!

ENGLISH: Yo, asshole! Get my bag now, or I'll fuckin' kill ya!
SPANISH: Jo, assholo! Gigame bolsa malet ahora o funckin su muerto!
FRENCH: Yovez, dierriezole! Grabon mon bagages ou vous fuchon mortez.
ITALIAN: Ay, asshollo! Getdado me bagali o fongu la matz! I morto!
GERMAN: Ja, ashenholongratzeimer! Getenzi mine suitgeben ach ein fuchenkiegelduchen! Killenchen!
SWAHILI: Jambo, behindili. Gesteili shanta kimepotea osake fuckiliilea!

PASSPORT & CUSTOMS:

—Okay, now let me look at your passport photo so I can have some belly laughs, too.
—You think my name is funny? In English, your name means "big stupid bird dropping."
—I thought you're supposed to search my clothing, not put it on.
—I have no idea how it got in there.
—Someone could've slipped it into my bag when I went to the W.C.
—Looks like foot powder in aluminum foil to me.
—Would you please tell your drug-sniffing dog to take his nose out of my fly?
—I was just going to ask you how much duty I have to pay on that.
—Where would your President leave a message for me?
—I'm here to discuss financing and operating a new airport.

—That's the most handsome uniform I've ever seen.
—Especially on you.
—You look too young to be working for your government.
—Are you sure you're not a movie star?
—I'm your dictator's American cousin.
—I'm here to study for the priesthood.
—A body-cavity search? What've I done? Can I do it to myself? While you watch, of course.
—This is my first body search. What's your sign?

BAGGAGE:

—When you find my bag, I'll give you back your hat.
—At twenty cents a scratch, you owe me $180.40.
—Could you hurry finding my baggage? I don't want to be late returning to the hospital for the criminally insane.
—Drop my bags one more time and I'll kill your dog!
—What's the biggest tip you've ever gotten—so far, that is?
—If I find out you lied and that I just tipped you four hundred dollars, I'll spend my whole vacation hunting for you.

MONEY EXCHANGE:

—Very funny. Now be serious.
—Do I look like I just got off the boat?
—Okay, what's the *real* exchange rate?
—Are you allowed to accept tips?
—In my country, seven times ten is seventy.
—I'm not laughing at the picture of your queen. I'm thinking of a funny joke.
—Now, use *my* calculator.
—Do you think this will be enough for my mother's brain tumor operation?
—The orphans will be so happy when I divide this among them.
—Now let's count them one at a time.

TAXIS:

—Lots of changes since I fought here to free your people.
—I can't believe they haven't fixed that pothole yet.
—Could you slow down? I just got out of the hospital.
—It feels so good not to have the police chasing me.
—The first day out of prison is always the best.
—I hope we get there before I need my antiviolent medicine.
—I've been holding in from throwing up all day.
—Say, didn't we share a prison cell for a few nights?
—[whispered slowly] The big red fox will eat the green moon
 tonight.
—Listen, pal, if we pass that one more time, the only way you're
 going to be able to read your meter is if you hold a mirror up
 your ass!

HOTEL:

—I know how to yell in your language "You want to suck my what?"
—Think of it this way—"My room or your life."
—I can't understand why your chief of police recommended I stay
 here.
—Do the initials "CIA" mean anything to you? How about "PLO"?
 How about "FU"?
—I'm here to cast a movie.
—Everything has been like a fairy tale since I won the lottery.
—My mother-in-law's rear end is a better view.
—Does that include my firstborn?
—I asked for my bill, not your national debt.
—Can the bellman come up before my suitcases go out of style?

EATING OUT:

—Just give me a hint. Did this originally have two or four legs and did it live on land or in water?

—In my country, they usually don't bring the animal to the table on a leash.

—Does the chef have long, curly black hair?

—Was anything on my plate in the movie *Bambi?*

—If you send my glass to a crime lab, I think you'll find out those are your fingerprints inside.

—Did you ever think of a career as a statue?

—I've seen people move faster in a Quaalude contest.

—Did you kill this chicken by throwing it into a fan?

—I hope my gravy didn't burn your fingers.

—I assume this word means "stomach pump."

—The only reason Michelin gave you three stars is because your food tastes like their tires.

—Is your chef doing an impression of a dog barking?

—Could I please have a knife, fork, hammer, and screwdriver?

—Do you accept American Express and Blue Cross?

—Where is your regurgitation room?

SIGHT-SEEING:

—Are you making all this up?

—Why did the other guide say sixteenth century?

—How much to let her in the church in shorts?

—Does the blessing come with a notarized guarantee?

—Don't you think Jesus would like us to spend more than three minutes in his birthplace?

—Don't you think nine dollars is a lot for a candle?

—Grab my wife's ass again, and I'll rip off your cheeks!

—Can we skip the cemetery and beer-malt factory?

—I don't give a flying crap who lived here.

—Your goat is eating my zipper.

—My guide is dead and they took my wife.

—Can I tie my shoe or is your water buffalo in heat?
—That's one helluva tattoo of a battleship. I had no idea your
women were so patriotic.

SHOPPING:

—Penicillin, please.
—More penicillin, please.
—How much? Are you crazy? Does it come with a slave?
—Down the street, it's half.
—I understood what you just said to him.
—If this doesn't arrive at my house in six days as promised, my
brother, who is staying on here, will staple your ears to your
head.
—Tell you what. You put it on, walk outside for five minutes, and if
no one laughs, I'll buy it.
—Tell me the truth, or I'll drop it.

MEDICAL:

—If it's my tooth, why are you shaving me there?
—Are you sure the garlic in the window will help?
—Do all your other patients have four legs?
—I prefer keeping my clothes on while you examine my ankle.
—Do I have to put on the paint and do the dance with you?
—Yes, I like whiskey, but I would prefer an anesthetic.
—Doctor, why do you also cut hair and fix shoes?
—As soon as you're finished, I'll let go of your testicles.
—Not your truck driver's license, your medical license.
—I have a rash the size of a large bedroom slipper.
—Is that your other patient baying?
—Since when does a rash have to be surgically removed?
—I still don't understand how you confused "vomiting" with "diar-
rhea."

—How many days before I take the cork out?
—Why do I have to take these pills at your uncle's bar?
—Could you put Vaseline on that, please?
—Don't you have the oral one?
—Is it necessary to have your whole family watch?
—Yes, I do mind holding your baby while you do this.
—Let me get this straight. First we collect bat wings. Then we take
  pig blood and mix it with the cobwebs from the top of a tree and
  put three night crawlers in a . . .
—Sorry, Doctor, you just startled me by jumping in here wearing
  that mask and waving that club.
—I'm not saying you're not a doctor. I simply refuse to have my
  hernia treated with leeches.

▼ ▼ ▼ Size 10D

It was one of those horrible red-eye, puddle-
hopper flights from San Francisco to New York. Every thirty-two feet
we landed. We stopped at McDonald's for a late snack. The worst.
From trying to squish myself into a semicomfortable position in my
seat, I was so bent out of shape, I had a nightmare that someone
was spreading mustard all over my skin and was about to take a big
bite out of me.

After we took off from Phoenix, I finally fell asleep, along with
the rest of the passengers. We set down at our next stop, I think it
was North Phoenix, and one passenger boarded, but from the noise
he made, one would think a family of twelve had joined us,
complete with their dogs, cats, and drums. He didn't talk to the
flight attendants—he bellowed. People with megaphone mouths

have always bothered me. My mother contended that you could tell the class of a person by their volume: the louder the voice, the lower the class. In the old neighborhood, loud people were called fishwives, so named for the women who hung around the docks hawking their fish. Well, this guy could've sold whales.

By the time he got to his seat, there wasn't a sleeping soul on the plane. After takeoff, he went to the bathroom, and I went for revenge.

My opportunity lay on the floor under the seat in front of him: his shoes. He had taken them off, with loud groans, of course, and tossed them there. His seat was diagonally across from mine. In the dimly lit cabin, I reached across the aisle and grabbed the shoes. Just in case there would be a body search by the police, I slipped them into the overnight bag of the priest sleeping next to me.

The noisemaker stomped his way back to his seat, complaining loudly about the rough quality of the face towels in the bathroom. Extracoarse sandpaper would have been too fine for this extra-coarse putz.

At the next stop, Barney Brouhaha stood, screamed to the flight attendant to bring him his jacket and overcoat, noisily retrieved his attaché from the overhead rack, and then bent over for his shoes. That's when the fun began.

At first he just jostled people about as he searched for his shoes. Then he screeched at the flight attendant that the plane would not take off again until she found his shoes. She suggested that sometimes during takeoff items slide backward, and vice versa upon landing. He demanded that all passengers search around their areas for his shoes. Those who did only did so, I'm certain, to get rid of the braying jackass.

I waited for a rare quiet moment before speaking.

"Excuse me, sir, but are you certain you were wearing shoes when you boarded?" I asked. The giggles began.

"Of course!" he screamed.

"Well, sir," I said, "I believe you're mistaken. I remember when you came on board because I was awakened by some kind of disturbance. I thought that upon landing we had hit a herd of elephants and they were crying out in pain. Anyway, I remember noticing you weren't wearing shoes and wondering why a well-dressed man such as yourself would be in his stocking feet, especially on such a cold night."

The passengers were hysterical. Even the crew laughed openly. Hippo Mouth glared at me. I could tell from his angry eyes that he knew that I had swiped his shoes, and he could tell from my eyes that there was no way I was going to return them. No way! He did the only thing he could do. He stormed off the plane to the wild and enthusiastic cheering of all on board.

The door closed. The plane took off. The lights were dimmed. I turned to the priest next to me, glancing obviously at his overnight bag and then back to him.

"Father," I whispered, "I'm sure you know some quiet and needy soul who wears a size ten-D."

"Bless you, my son," he said, laughing.

▲ ▲ ▲ Drive Carefully

Am I alone or are there others who hate when they are leaving someone's house or apartment and the person says, "Drive carefully"? Am I the only one who, upon hearing this advice, feels like running over their cat, smashing through their garage door, careening across their backyard, flattening their sun-tanning grandmother, and then crashing through their fence, smiling and waving good-bye and driving away as though nothing had happened? Carefully, of course.

◇ ◇ ◇ **Dying for Profit**

I traveled extensively when I was a television documentary filmmaker. As I was preparing to leave my office for a trip one day, a fellow producer jokingly asked me to buy a flight-insurance policy with him as my beneficiary. I said I'd gladly do it and took his dollar to buy it. This was the beginning of a scam I pulled off for many years.

Whenever I was booked on a flight, I would collect money from my coworkers for flight-insurance policies naming them the beneficiaries. Some thought it was ghoulish, but profit trumps ghoulish. I averaged between seventy-five and a hundred dollars per trip for about thirty to forty trips per year. Of course, by not buying one policy, it was all profit. Why should I buy one? When I lived, no one expected to collect money, and if I died in a crash, what the hell could they do to me for ripping them off?

One person asked why he never received a copy of the insurance policy in the mail, to which I quickly and convincingly replied, "Would you trust the U.S. mail with that much of your money? I mail the policy to my lawyer, who has instructions to contact you when I crash and burn." I think it was the "crash and burn" that stopped any further questioning.

If you are one of the persons I conned in my youth, I have included you in my will for a nice chunk of money. My lawyer will contact you.

★ ★ ★ **Never Too Safe**

My brother and I were sitting in the London airport waiting for our flight back home. Seated next to me was a beautiful girl of about age nine or ten. She had wonderfully smooth brown skin, shiny pitch-black hair, and eyes to match. We exchanged smiles. I could tell that someday she would be a great beauty. Around the time I would be a great white prune.

Suddenly the girl leapt to her feet and ran across the airport and into the arms of a dark-skinned woman. They hugged and kissed so excitedly, and with arms wrapped tightly around each other, they headed for the exit. What a wonderful scene to remember, I thought.

I watched them until they left the airport and then turned away. It was then that I noticed that in all the excitement, the little girl had forgotten her little suitcase. I could still catch her. I leaned down to pick up the suitcase and froze when I noticed that the writing on the name tag was in Arabic. I grabbed my brother's arm, pulling him to his feet.

"Let's go, Moby," I called out.

"What? What's up?"

"Just follow me. It's serious!"

He could tell I was troubled, so without another word he hurried with me to the uniformed bobby some twenty yards away.

I quickly told the police officer about the little girl and my suspicion that she had left a bomb. Just as I finished, I saw the little girl come running back into the airport. Her mother stood just inside the door, smiling as she watched her daughter retrieve her suitcase and come running back. They both laughed and again left with their arms around one another.

"I feel like a real idiot, Officer."

"You shouldn't, guv. Nowadays, you can never be too safe."

I'm sorry to say that the officer is right. Such are the times in which we live. Sad, isn't it?

HOTELS & RESTAURANTS

★ ★ ★ ★ ★ ★ ★ ★ ★ ★ ★ ★

More Things You Hate to See

- The man you yelled at in the airport is now standing behind the desk of your hotel.

- The entire roll of toilet paper has been folded into a point.

- Insects crawling along the toilet sanitation strip.

- Oxygen mask hanging from the ceiling over your bed.

- The wake-up clock is not nailed down, but the sheets are.

- Room service number is the same as bus station coffee shop.

- On the bathroom mirror, written in lipstick, is "Call police."

- Sign nailed to the back of the door reads CALL MANAGER IF YOU SMELL SMOKE OR A JEW.

- Room rates posted on the door are only by the hour and half hour.

- When you come out of your shower and walk into the bedroom naked, the chambermaid is naked in your bed.

- Inside the pillow—feathers; inside the feathers—a duck.

- All other guests have large humps on their backs.

- The green ring around the inside of your tub then goes along the wall, down the hall, around the lobby, and across the street.

- From your window you see the hotel that was pictured on the cover of the brochure.

- Heimlich maneuver instructions on the cover of the restaurant menu.

- Under your napkin is an airsick bag.

- Your waiter in the kitchen picking his nose.

- The chef scratching his ass.

- Your waiter picking your chef's nose and your chef scratching your waiter's ass.

- Chef's suggestion on the menu is the name of a different restaurant.

◆ ◆ ◆ Gulliver Slept Here

I'm sure you've heard stories about the demands show business people make about their accommodations when they travel. Only brown M&M candies in the dressing room, four freshly killed chickens to cook, only French Impressionist paintings on the walls, firecrackers to light and toss, a foam-rubber toilet seat, a four-legged bathtub, a pink Mercedes-Benz stretch limo, and other ridiculous things. Mine are very simple. I'm allergic to feathers, so I need foam pillows; and I have a bad back and am six feet two inches tall, so I need a king-size bed.

Most hotels are used to having celebrities and take them as they come, which is what I prefer. But, in some of the smaller communities, people get excited and make a fuss over you. In the lobby of a hotel in New Hampshire, my manager and I were met by an entourage that included the general manager, day manager, public relations director, director of food and beverages, head of housekeeping, concierge, and two bellmen. I assumed the last performer to stay there was Al Jolson.

We crowded onto the elevator and rode up to our floor. The suite was very nice and was filled with fresh cut flowers, complimentary chilled champagne, hot hors d'oeuvres, fresh coffee, and a basket of fruit. There was a VCR with a good selection of movies. I thanked everyone and shook their hands. They insisted that we see the bedroom.

It looked like any hotel bedroom, except for the bed. As usual, we'd told the hotel that if they didn't have a king-size bed to just put two beds together, which is what they did—only they did it foot to foot instead of side to side. The result was a bed twelve feet long with a headboard at each end. I thought it was a joke, but no one was laughing.

I said, "Who's the putz who put the beds together like this?"

"I am," confessed the general manager meekly.

I laughed and put my arm around his shoulder. "Did you think that when I toss and turn, I do it longways, rolling twelve feet forward and then twelve feet backward?"

By this time, everyone was laughing, including the mastermind of the longest bed in New England.

The next morning, when I was checking out, I was asked to sign their guest book. I wrote, "I had a wonderful time in Lilliput. Thank you. Your friend, Gulliver."

► ► ► **Checkout Time**

You should check out of your hotel if:

- people in the town commit suicide by jumping *into* the hotel.
- they advertise that George Washington *would've* slept there.
- they advertise that George Washington is still sleeping there.
- you put a quarter in the bedside magic-fingers vibrator and only one finger works, and it's the one in the middle.
- you can't identify the origin of more than half of the marks and stains in the room.
- it was listed as a four-star hotel and you find out that the four stars are Rudy Vallee, Fibber McGee, Hoot Gibson, and Fatty Arbuckle.
- you're the only one in the lobby not wearing short shorts and fishnet stockings.
- on the wall behind the desk is a portrait of Calvin Coolidge.
- the concierge is wearing only an undershirt.
- the room-service number has a long-distance prefix.
- you are handed a skeleton key for your door.
- the hotel dick is exposing his.
- they are holding cockfights in the lobby.

- the bellhop has no arms.
- in the hall you smell formaldehyde.
- the DO NOT DISTURB is a chicken foot with a black ribbon wrapped around it hanging from a string.
- the lumps in your mattress move.
- if you threw up on the rug, no one would notice it.
- someone has left his feet outside his door to be shined.
- to call the operator you dial 98767876223435667809875660l.
- they hand you a quill pen to sign the register.
- the last name on the register is Manson, Charles.
- the night manager's name is Norman Bates.
- when you talk to the desk clerk, you hear an echo.
- there's half a wrecking ball sticking through the wall of your room.
- there's a picture of Manuel Noriega on the wall of your room.
- someone stole Jesus from the crucifix above your bed.
- someone stole half of Jesus from the crucifix above your bed.
- someone replaced Jesus with Happy the Clown.
- the Gideon's Genesis begins, "Okay, here's what happened the first day . . ."
- the towels are from another hotel.
- your room is 1407 and the one next to you is 2614.
- when you look into the bathroom mirror, you see the back of your head.
- the face soap is in the shape of a chicken's spleen.
- it *is* a chicken's spleen.
- the health club is full of sick people.
- wounded RAF pilots are in beds in the hallways.
- a ski lift runs through your room.
- there are thick pads on the walls.
- the people at the bar all have shotguns.
- the restaurant has paper plates and plastic utensils and cardboard waitresses.
- when you ask the cashier to change a dollar, she changes it into a quarter.
- the lobby phone is on the ceiling and someone is using it.
- when you ask the doorman to call you a cab, that's what he calls you.

- the doorman's cap reads "Doeman."
- when you turn off the light switch, the room is still brightly lit.
- when you flick out the lights, the room gets brighter.
- there's a flashing red light outside your bedroom window, and it's a man holding a flashing red light.
- everyone else on your floor is getting fifty dollars an hour.
- your bed squeaks when you're not in it.
- when you turn on your faucet, your bed gets wet.
- when you turn off your faucet, your bed explodes.
- when you get into bed, the faucet turns on.
- the thing that went bang in the night was the night watchman's head.
- in the middle of the night, actors enter your room and play out the life of Eva Braun.
- the flowers in the wallpaper are dead.
- the TV is black and blue.
- when you press the channel changer, the toilet blows up.
- the TV is steam operated.
- the ceiling is four feet high.
- when you pull the toilet chain, the room flushes.
- the happy hour begins at six A.M.
- you don't want to steal the towels.
- the medicine cabinet is jammed with medicines.
- during the night, you gain a lot of weight.
- the couch folds out into a lobster trap.
- when you turn out your lights, you can see into the next room.
- moss is growing in the corners.
- the bathwater is dusty.
- the maintenance man fixes your air conditioner with a leg of lamb.
- when you ask for the bill, they hand you a bird's beak.
- to get telephone information, you have to yell down the stairs.
- when you tip the bellhop a dollar, he drops to his knees and kisses your feet.
- the town funeral director introduces himself to you.

▼ ▼ ▼ **What's Your Sign?**

Small hanging breasts up ahead

A funny thing is going to happen to you on the way there

Taxi stand ahead

Evangelist ahead

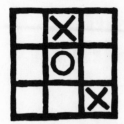

Your move

Giraffe crossing

Spanish information booth

You're almost there

▼ ▼ ▼ **Thank You, Mr. President**

It was the best suite in the best hotel in town. It had everything you would ever need or want, and then some. Three king-size bedrooms, a huge living room with a giant-screen TV, a twelve-chair dining room, a conference room for sixteen, a completely stocked bar, three other TVs, five and a half bathrooms, three large Jacuzzis, marble floors and thick carpets, remote-controlled blackout blinds, baskets of complimentary snacks, and three dozen telephones whose wires were all over the floor like snakes in molting.

Why all the phones? I'll give you a moment to think about it. . . . Give up? So did I, so I called the front desk and was informed that President Reagan had checked out of the suite just that morning, after a stay of a few days. I should have put two and two together when I saw the brown hair-dye stains in the master bathroom sink. The phones were used by his staff. I had hoped he was going to tell me that Ronnie and Nancy were huge "TV Shopper's Market" fans. I asked him to please remove the phones, and he said he'd call me back. I asked him on which phone, so I wouldn't feel as if I were in a Three Stooges movie. He said on the hotel phone I was using.

As I waited, I thought how this was the only time I had stayed in a presidential suite in which a President had actually stayed.

I decided to test the phones. I picked up about twenty of them and they all had dial tones. Then I saw it: the red phone. *The* red phone. Oh, my God, this was the baby that led right into the War Room, the Pentagon, the CIA, or the Kremlin. I could start World War Three, put a hit out on Arafat or Qaddafi, or at least, get the IRS off my back about my tax shelters.

I decided there was probably some kind of code that had to be pressed or a switch that had to be thrown or the phone would blow you into oblivion. Then I remembered how the President sometimes forgot what country he was visiting, so there is no way anyone would count on him to remember a secret code. I picked up the phone and listened. There was a normal-sounding dial tone, not a mechanical "Hail to the Chief." I listened for some kind of click indicating the phone was being tapped. Nothing. What the hell. I dialed 411.

"May I help you?"

By absolutely blind luck, I had reached the contact.

"The Kremlin," I replied authoritatively.

"One moment, please."

I couldn't believe it. I started to hang up but then thought that maybe with a one-on-one, man-to-man talk, I could work out world peace.

Comedian David Brenner Gets Peace Agreement on All Points During a Casual Chat with Soviet Premier

"Sir?"

"Yes." My heart jumped.

"Do you want the Kremlin Laundromat or Pizza House?"

Obviously some kind of password question. I took a wild stab at it.

"The Kremlin the President always calls."

"Which president, sir?"

Obviously a trick question devised by the CIA to catch any unauthorized person trying to use the hot line. Having read enough about our CIA, I shot back a reply.

"The President of the United States of America."

"One moment, please."

I knew I could break the CIA code.

"Sir, you can reach the President by calling the White House in Washington, DC. Do you wish me to connect you to Washington information?"

Well, well, well, the CIA was trickier than I thought. I had better spend some time working this out.

"No, thanks, I'll dial it directly."

"Fine, sir," she said, adding haltingly, "Have a terrific evening."

"You, too."

I hung up and took out a pad and pencil. I was a cryptographer in the army and was good at breaking codes. Let's see. The woman said, "Have a terrific evening," instead of the rote, "Have a nice day." Hmmmmmmmm. *Have* starts with an *h*. I wrote the first letter of each word and had the key. H-A-T-E. *Hate*. But what does it mean? Does Reagan hate the Kremlin? Should I hate the Kremlin? Does the President hate me? My thoughts were interrupted by the phone's ringing.

"Hello. Hate."

"What?"

It was the night manager.

"Oh, sorry, I was just thinking about liver. I hate liver. So, what's up?"

"Well, Mr. Brenner, I contacted the local phone man who helped install the phones in your suite, and he told me that the CIA authorized and supervised the installation and would have to do the same for removing them."

"So when is the CIA coming over? I have to shower soon to get ready for my opening-night show."

"Well, Mr. Brenner—"

"Call me David, please."

"Thank you, Mr. Brenner. Well, David, the problem is that it is Friday evening and the CIA offices won't be open until Monday morning."

"In other words, spies from foreign countries who are in America just wait until the weekend to go to work because our boys are mowing their lawns."

"I don't know very much about spies, I'm afraid."

"They have big, red cheeks from laughing at the CIA. Okay, then just send up your maintenance man to rip out the phones and you can mail them to Washington on Monday."

"I'm afraid I can't do that. They are federal government property, and—"

"Come on, it looks like Medusa had her hair cut in here. You mean I'm going to have to crawl around all these wires until at least Monday?"

"I'm afraid so. Sorry."

"It's not your fault. Thanks for trying. Good night."

"Thanks and have a terrific engagement, Mr. . . . David."

I hung up. The plot was really getting thick and gooey. The night manager's last words: "Have a terrific engagement." There it was again. H.A.T.E. Was it a secret branch of the CIA? Maybe a covert operation? I decided to work on it, after I unpacked.

When I tossed my phone directory on the bed, it fell open to the Z's. Only my business manager's last name starts with Z. I thought how he was in London seeing another client and a few plays and . . . wait a minute. If the CIA won't remove the phones, then they should be used. I H.A.T.E. federal government waste.

I spoke to Bill Z. for only a few minutes because I had to get ready for my show. However, later that night, we finished the conversation, and then we hooked up a conference call with my attorney, who was vacationing in Portugal.

That weekend I called all my Los Angeles friends, a few people who had befriended me in Australia, a couple in Japan I had met, all the members of my family, and everyone I knew, everywhere in the world. In between these conversations, I called a sailboat manufacturer in Italy for specs on a boat they were building, the Louvre Museum to find out their present show, weather in all European capitals, a former sailing captain whom I tracked down off the coast of east Africa, the international maritime operator, who connected me to some of my favorite ocean liners, the curator at the Cairo Museum to inquire whether the King Tut exhibition would be returning to the USA, and even managed to get through to Scotland Yard, to whom I volunteered my services should they ever need an American contact.

The only call I tried to make and didn't get through was to the CIA. They really were closed for the weekend. Well, I never did get through to the Kremlin, but I did decipher the code word *HATE*, so if anyone from the CIA reads this and plans to come after me to pay the phone bill, I'll go to the press and spill the beans.

▲   ▲   ▲   # No Clinks, No Clanks

Don't despair when you are put into a hotel room that has a row of vending and ice machines directly outside your door. Don't fight with management about changing your room and then get depressed when they don't. Matter of fact, don't even complain. Do what I do. Unpack the pad of stickers you had printed. You know, the ones that read OUT OF ORDER. Now, simply go out into the hall and put a sticker over each coin slot. Remember to remove them when you check out. After all, fair is fair.

◇   ◇   ◇   # The Commodian

Explain this one to me, if you can. Who decided to put full-length mirrors on the inside of bathroom doors directly across from the commode? I don't care how good-looking you are, an Adonis or Venus de Milo, there is no way you look good sitting on the john. Even the most narcissistic person cannot possibly enjoy the view. Was it simply someone's brilliant idea for humbling all travelers? If it was, it works, for me anyway.

Here's another one for you: Who decided that the bottom sheet of toilet paper should be folded into the shape of a point and sealed with a gold sticker? For fun, whenever I am staying in a hotel for a week or longer, every time I use the toilet paper, I refold it into the point and put the gold sticker back on. After about five days, whenever I leave my hotel room, I can see the housekeeping staff looking quizzically at me and whispering to each other. I can just imagine what they are saying:

"That's him. Seven-B. Nine days. He never goes to the bathroom."

"Why, that's David Brenner."

"How can he be so funny all stuffed up like that?"

The other thing I do is buy rolls of toilet paper and unroll them into different degrees, from two sheets remaining to only two sheets used. The first day, I take the "real" hotel roll off and replace it with the half-used roll. The next day we are down to less than a quarter of a roll, but somehow, miraculously, on the third day, the roll is full again, but oh, my God, it is down again to almost out, but it makes an amazing comeback and . . . etc. You can imagine the housekeeping discussions with this one.

As a tall person (six two), I must register a complaint against 99.9 percent of the hotels in the world. I have spent my adult life contorting in a Quasimodo shape in order to get my hair wet in the shower or see my face in the medicine cabinet mirror. I guess the union allows no one over five six to install shower heads and medicine cabinets in hotels.

How about this weird one. In gambling towns in the United States, the tissue boxes are locked into the wall. Meanwhile, millions of dollars in chips and cash are in the wide open within anyone's reach. Even by the little guy who put the shower heads in the bathroom of the hotel. Are they really fearful that one night a gang of masked men with guns are going to rush into the casino and yell, "We don't want your money! Just bust open all the Kleenex boxes or we'll kill ya!"

Most confusing to me is that paper strip that hotels slip over the toilet seat FOR YOUR CONVENIENCE AND PROTECTION. First of all, what is so convenient about sitting on that piece of paper? And protection against what? I was never attacked by a toilet seat in my life. Never! And if those little strips of paper really could protect, people would be wearing them around their heads.

★ ★ ★ **Three on a Match**

In my late teens, I was a soldier stationed in Germany. I loved being a teenager and hated being a soldier, so, every chance I got, I'd travel around Europe. This was very often, because a friend of mine kept track of leave time for my battalion. Thanks to my good fortune playing poker, I was able to keep a garret room at 44 Rue du Madam on the Left Bank in Paris. I went there whenever the fancy struck me—and with a teen libido, the fancy struck often.

Late one night, as I was exiting my attic room to go to the bathroom at the end of the hall, I saw a couple in their early thirties walking up the steps. The woman was leading the way, carrying only her purse. The man, a couple steps below her, was struggling with four heavy suitcases, three of which were matching.

The woman was pissed off. The man was pissed *on.* They were definitely Americans, and from the look of the situation, they were married. When the wife reached the landing, she stopped and wiped the few beads of perspiration from her brow. The husband was still on the stairs and unable to mop the flood of sweat from his face. She took out a cigarette, looked at me, and spoke loudly and slowly as one does when addressing a foreigner.

"Got . . . a . . . match?"

I disliked this woman immediately because I have always had disdain for domineering or loud people, and she was both. I shrugged as though I didn't understand. Her face soured even more.

"Fire! Fire!" she screamed, waving her cigarette in my face.

Again I shrugged, adding a puzzled expression on my face and a shake of my head.

Sourpuss exploded. "Fire! Burn! . . . Hot! . . . Eh . . . oh, for Christ sake these Frenchmen are so stupid! What the hell's he think I want?"

I whipped out my United States Army–issue Zippo lighter, flicked on the flame, and shoved it in her face.

"Ya wanna light, lady?"

She was livid but only jammed the cigarette in her twisted lips and pushed the tip into the fire. As she puffed, I looked at her husband. He had the smile of the man who broke the bank at Monte Carlo. He gave me a big wink. He would probably still be standing there smiling and winking if, instead of giving his wife a light, I would've shoved her down the stairs, but she was his problem and the midnight boulevards of Paris were awaiting.

◆ ◆ ◆ Money Talks in the Morning

I admit that I am one of the world's most paranoid people. Whenever I have to awaken in the morning for something important, I am positive my alarm won't work and the hotel operator will forget my wake-up call. This drove me crazy for years, until I came up with the foolproof, money-talks wake-up. Here's the thought process that went into creating it.

This involves having a totally reliable person call you exactly when you want to be called. Now who is one hundred percent dependable? Someone who will benefit from your waking up on time. Who would benefit? Someone who will make a lot of money. Who could that be? *Voilà!*

I call a local real estate broker and tell him I am interested in purchasing for cash a total of 200,000 square feet of office space. Because I am pressed for time, if he calls me at exactly eight A.M. the next morning, I'll tell him when I can meet with him.

As a backup, I always use a furrier whom I'll meet to see the $80,000 white Russian sable coat.

▶ ▶ ▶ # H.H. Himself

There is a huge and beautiful hotel in Acapulco, and I recommend it highly. However, for anyone trying to get away from the crowds and out of the spotlight, it is the wrong place to go. I didn't know this and went there for the five days I had off between a six-week tour of mostly one-nighters that had just ended and a three-week Las Vegas engagement that was coming up next. I was seeking peace and tranquillity, no show-biz buzz, just surf and sun, food and fun.

Everyone had told me this hotel was beautiful, and it was, but no one had informed me that it was the size of a small city. I knew I was going to have problems the minute I saw that all the women at the pool were wearing gold jewelry and thick makeup. I took a lounge at the farthest point from the pool, near bushes and in the shade. I figured everyone wanted to get a tan and show off their diamonds and gold and wouldn't come anywhere near there, but I was wrong.

Before I even had a chance to drape the towel on the back of the lounge, I was surrounded by a small group of bejeweled women ranging in ages from forty-eight to forty-nine who were asking—no, make that *demanding*—autographs for this daughter and that son, or this neighbor or this son-in-law and that daughter-in-law and this jeweler or that jeweler.

As I usually do, I courteously signed my name to whatever they handed me, ranging in this case from high-heeled shoes to beach balls, and I listened to all these wonderfully exciting stories about all the celebrities they had met, where they saw them, what they were wearing, what they said, how nice or bitchy they were, and their analyses of why their careers were zooming, fading, or over. After a half hour of nonstop signing, I excused myself to go to the bathroom, figuring anyone vacationing in Mexico would understand.

In the lobby, I signed a few dozen more autographs. The indoor crowd was older, so the autographs were for grandchildren, bridge partners, proctologists, and pharmacists, and the stories about celebrities were of those you either see on "Love Boat" or in new wallets, or both.

On the elevator, I was lucky, running into only one fan. Unfortunately, she had four children and eight grandchildren.

As soon as I closed the door of my suite, I poured a drink and flopped down on the couch. Now, I want to make it clear that I really don't mind signing autographs. As a matter of fact, I only refused to sign once. It was a young woman in a disco who was drunk and caustic. Actually, I did sign her paper cocktail napkin, but then, after a particularly bigoted remark, I stuffed it into her drink. The only time I don't sign immediately is when I'm eating. I ask the person to either leave the paper, which I'll sign as soon as I finish my meal, or to return when they see I'm done. This was after more than a decade of eating cold food that started out hot. I really appreciate people's asking me for my autograph, because I have always believed it is their way of thanking you for the pleasure you have given them. It is a very small price to pay for the wonderful life show business has given me. However, after six weeks of nightly performances all over the country, I really wanted and needed to mellow out and recharge my batteries. For five days, I wanted to be a person, not a celebrity.

The suite in which I was staying was a fine example of the benefits one derives from a show-business career. It was one of the largest and most lavish suites I had ever seen, but for me, it had turned into a trap. If I stepped out of it, I was onstage. I knew I had to check out of the hotel, and pronto.

I called my travel agent, Ronnie, and requested alternatives.

"Ronnie, try to book me in another hotel in Acapulco, or rent me a house here, or get me a room in another part of Mexico, or book me in a resort close to Mexico, or send me to a small hotel, motel, house, single room, bungalow, boardinghouse, or a private room in a hospital anywhere in the world where I can get one hundred and twenty hours of peaceful time all to myself."

Ronnie got the point. She would call me back. If anyone could do it, she could. She's the best. I began to relax.

Then the phone rang. After hanging up fifteen minutes later, I called the operator and asked her to please screen my calls so I wouldn't have to listen to another Sophie from Yonkers who thinks her neighbor Bella's third cousin Ruthie is related to me through her bubby's half sister's brother, Yonkel, the baker who made such a nice wedding for his daughter Elka's daughter, Faith, and she would simply die, God forbid, if she didn't bring an autograph home to her grandson, Josh, who already has Soupy Sales's autograph, whom she met at a B'nai B'rith benefit. Who could refuse? I said I'd leave it at the front desk and apologized for not being able to accept her invitation to join her and her Saul for a small bite, a wonderful husband for forty-seven years. I'll spare you the story of his triple bypass. I hung up and waited more desperately than ever for Ronnie's call.

The next time the phone rang, I answered it in a very bad nasal-drip, sinus-headache, French accent.

"Hi, David," responded my travel agent immediately. "I found you a place where you could get rid of that terrible cold and terrible French accent." I knew she would come through.

She booked me into a suite in a hotel across town. Each suite had its own private swimming pool, so by ordering room service, I could avoid seeing another human being until I checked out for the airport. Perfect.

I was packed and out of my suite in thirty seconds. It would've been fifteen, but the chambermaid had lived in L.A. for six months and was a big fan of the "Tonight Show" and . . . you can fill in the blanks.

The clerk at the front desk was very cordial, but he couldn't understand why I was checking out. He tried his best to get me to reconsider, but I countered every reason he gave for staying. Then he leaned on the front counter and signaled me to come closer. I did. He looked around and over his shoulder. I figured the next thing would be about a new mushroom that causes visions of huge, multicolored breasts floating in a sea of naked women. I was wrong.

"Señor Brenner," he whispered, "I don't think you know where you are staying."

I whispered back, "Don't tell me this is Hadassah headquarters?"

He didn't know what the hell I was talking about, so we were even.

"Señor Brenner, H.H. Himself died in the very bed in the very room in which you are staying."

"I thought Hubert Humphrey died in Wisconsin?"

"The H.H. Himself."

"The H.H. Himself?" I repeated.

He nodded.

I nodded.

He nodded again.

This was getting ridiculous. I was going to spend the better portion of my short vacation playing nodding Ping-Pong, but I was curious to find out who *the* H.H. Himself was.

"I heard that one of H.H. Himself's last requests was that after his death he never be referred to as H.H. Himself."

"I never heard that, señor. For security reasons, we at the hotel always referred to H.H. . . . eh, to Howard Hughes, as H.H."

Of course, now I remembered the whole story of how he was rushed by chopper from his hotel suite to a hospital in Texas in a failed attempt to save his life. I signaled the clerk to come closer. When he did, I looked around and over my shoulders. I whispered very softly.

"Do you think that the fact that an eccentric who saved his urine in bottles and had toenails that broke furniture when he walked, that because he died in the very bed I'm to sleep in, that is a good enough reason for me to stay here? If you do, then you'd better buy a few thousand bottles and throw away your shoes, because you are crazier than he was. Now, *por favor,* señor, my bill and a taxi, pronto."

After putting away the last of my clothes in my delightfully secluded little "house suite" at my new hotel, I dove naked into my private pool. The only time I signed my name during the next five days was on my American Express charge slip when I was checking out. What a fabulous vacation.

Viva Mexico! *Viva* H.H. Himself!

▼ ▼ ▼ My Favorite Flying Joke

When I heard this one, I cracked up about it for days. Every time I think about it, it knocks me out. I'm laughing already. Okay, here it goes: The flight attendant announces to the passengers that "the first person to slide down the emergency chute will stay at the bottom and help the other passengers."

Doesn't that just kill you? And if you aren't the first one down, it probably will.

▶ ▶ ▶ Water, Water Everywhere

What's the first thing that comes to mind when you think of Mexico? *Don't drink the water!* I am not one to ignore tips from seasoned travelers or sufferers, so, when I vacationed South of the Border, I was determined not to fall victim to Montezuma's Revenge.

I was so smart, I even impressed myself. Not only did I drink only bottled water, but I used it to wash out the glass from which I drank. Then I made certain to request all bottled drinks without ice. Can you imagine some schmuck pouring a safe drink over ice made from the local water? I used bottled water to wash my plates and silverware and brush my teeth. I remembered to keep my mouth shut in the shower. If I didn't personally peel the fruit or vegetables, I didn't eat them. I avoided everything that was made with water, from soup to sherbet. I covered all the bases, and it worked.

No one with me went to such extremes. Matter of fact, some of them took no precautions whatsoever and miraculously never got sick. Pure luck. Well, I believe you have to work for your luck, so I let others' laughter slide off my back and never let down my guard and had a fantastic and healthy time in a wonderfully hospitable and interesting country.

It wasn't until my twenty-fourth straight hour of sitting on my toilet at home that I figured it out. The plane from Acapulco to New York stocked its ice in Mexico. *Mexican ice!* Therefore, the Bloody Marys I had on the way home to toast my not getting sick in Mexico were loaded with little, square, frozen Montezuma time bombs.

Conclusion: Some schmucks are born on the way home.

SIGHT-SEEING

◀ ◀ ◀ ◀ ◀ ◀ ◀ ◀ ◀ ◀ ◀ ◀ ◀

◊ ◊ ◊ # Wish You Were Here

I hate buying, writing, mailing, and receiving postcards. It's my vacation. Why should I be taking some of this hard-earned, all-too-fleeting time to look through spinning racks of picture postcards, to say nothing of writing and mailing them? Besides, let's face it, most of the pictures look nothing like the place you're visiting, right? Your hotel is not in the middle of an open field; it is in the middle of a field of other hotels. The bright blue sky and radiant, yellow sun were airbrushed in. Or else the pictures are so old that the little kids are wearing pompadours and all the women look like the Andrews Sisters. Of course there are shots of nude and seminude women who look absolutely nothing like any woman you have seen in that country but an awful lot like the postcards in the last few countries you were in. Then there are the humorous ones, such as the bullfighter looking aghast at what the bull has sticking on the end of his horn. Ouch!

Why then do people send postcards? To show that they remember their loved ones still at home? Bull. Who forgets his family and friends when he goes away for two weeks? The real reason you send postcards is to rub it in. It is your sadistic way of saying that you are having a fantastic time swimming and sunning in paradise while your poor schmuck friends and relatives are busting their humps at work.

149

If people send me postcards, I send them one when I travel—to get even. I write things like "This is the diamond capital of the world and I want to get you one, but don't know if you like pear- or heart-shaped. Please call me next week at my hotel in Paris at . . ." It is at this point that I either rip the card, as if a post office machine somewhere destroyed the information, or I write the information and then smear it with a wet washrag, as though the card got caught in the rain. Sometimes, I obliterate everything on the card, so they have no idea who wrote them what from where.

There is really only one totally honest postcard. The picture is of you having the happiest time of your life, giving the finger, and on the other side is written:

Dear Doris and Ted:

Wish you weren't here and you're not. Wish I were here and I am.

Up yours,

★ ★ ★ **The Old Man and the Road**

I whipped the Alfa Romeo Spider convertible around another bend in the mountain road. Elizabeth and I were on our way back to Marbella from a day trip to a delightful little Spanish town called Coín. Limping along the road was a man in his late seventies. I moved the car over so I wouldn't cover him with dust and whipped by him.

"David, stop and pick up that man."

"He didn't fall."

"Come on, David, I'm serious."

"You're nuts."

"He must be almost eighty years old and he's limping."

"A lot of people his age limp."

"Don't be funny. I'm serious."

I stopped the car.

"Listen, I'm not picking up the old man and I'll tell you why. Think for a second. Why is an old man with a limp walking down a mountain road? We didn't pass a dead donkey or a car out of gas, or a broken bicycle, did we? The old man must be off. Maybe he's a psycho who just came out of the woods after escaping from some Spanish insane asylum. Maybe he's limping because he hurt his leg kicking to death the last couple who picked him up. Maybe he has a shotgun or a chain saw down his pants leg. Uh-oh, Jasono is getting closer."

I threw the car into first gear.

"David, he looks so tired. Please."

"Damn."

I put the gearshift into reverse and backed up to the old man, my hand on the door handle, so I could swing it open and knock him off the mountain if he suddenly opened his fly to grab the handle of the shotgun or saw or whatever. He smiled a toothless smile. So? Mass murderers don't smile?

With my limited Spanish, I asked if he wanted a ride. He smiled even wider. Not one tooth. At least he wasn't a vampire. He thanked me graciously over and over. He started to look more harmless. I made another offer to drive him home. This time he laughed and thanked me profusely. I said good-bye and waved as I drove away.

Approximately sixty feet down the road, there was another bend. I maneuvered around it and was in a small town. The old man's small town. No wonder he was laughing so much. Two crazy Americans were trying to drive him all the way home, all sixty feet. We passed an outdoor café where there were about a dozen old men sitting.

"David, stop the car. Let's pick up all the old men and take them home with us."

"Very funny."

"Then how about having a drink at the café with them?"

"No way."

"Why not?"

"Didn't you notice? Everyone has no teeth and limps. It's probably a local disease and highly contagious."

In the rearview mirror, I saw our original old man join the others. He pointed to our car as he spoke. They laughed. We waved.

◆ ◆ ◆ Signs of Our Times

I always get a big kick out of formally printed signs that are supposed to be serious. There really is something about them that makes no sense at all.

One of the most frightening signs to me is the one on a bridge that reads MAXIMUM LOAD 5 TONS. As I am halfway across the bridge, I see a large truck coming toward me and roughly calculate, including its cargo, that it would weigh in at around three tons. Therefore, the bridge and I are quite safe. I relax. Then I look in my rearview mirror and see the grille of a double tractor-trailer bearing down on me, weighing in at about four tons or more. Conclusion: Within thirty seconds, I'll be swimming around in the backseat of my car.

I'd like to discover the identity of the idiot who decided to put on the back of a flatbed truck transporting an entire house at a maximum speed downhill of seven miles per hour, the signs WIDE LOAD and SLOW-MOVING VEHICLE.

One of the most ponderable signs to me has been NO ROAD REPAIR WITHOUT A PERMIT. Now, I don't know about you, but sometimes at night, especially when I'm unable to sleep, I like to get out that old pneumatic drill, a shovel, and bucket of hot pitch and drive out to a nearby highway and fill in some of those nasty potholes. Guess the fun is over.

I'm not sure how you feel about this, but when I've been behind the wheel of a car nonstop for hours with my bladder about to explode, and I pull into a gasoline station, driving as close to the rest room as possible without causing structural damage, I am delighted to see a sign on the door reading LOCKED FOR YOUR CONVENIENCE. Really, what is more convenient in life than running cross-legged to the attendant to get the key?

Why do they put on gasoline self-service pumps REMOVE HOSE? Are there really people out there who would press the handle, watch a full tank of gasoline run down the pump and across the ground, and then pay for it?

On vending machines, why do they put a sign reading INSERT ONE (1) QUARTER? If someone is too stupid to be able to read "one," how will they be able to understand "insert"?

I steer clear of any roadside restaurant that displays a sign like GOOD FOOD SINCE 1986, because I always wonder what the food was like before that date, and worry that they might have slipped back into their old ways of cooking.

In a fine restaurant in Manhattan was a huge sign covering a wall that read FOR BATHROOM USE STAIRCASE—and in New York, they will.

One of the dumbest signs in America is a federal government sign that is plastered on billboards across our highways. It reads: ILLITERATE? CALL 1-800 . . .

There is a convent atop a hill in California, the grounds of which take up a square city block. Around this magnificent complex is a high, iron fence on which there is a sign even bigger than the fence itself. I drove around the block because I thought my eyes were playing tricks on me. The sign read NO TRESPASSING! TRESPASSERS WILL BE PROSECUTED TO THE FULL EXTENT OF THE LAW! and beneath it, SISTERS OF MERCY.

The ultimate funny sign one can see when traveling is FREE. Sure.

More Things You Hate to Hear

- You must've gotten on the bus just as I was changing the sign.
- Maybe many, many years ago.
- That was the old owner.
- Didn't you know this is our monsoon season?
- What pool?
- What suites?
- What beach?
- What reservation?
- What?
- Ha-ha-ha-ha-ha-ha-ha-ha-ha . . .
- I baggage help porter you room asparagus bank.
- We believe we found part of your suitcase.
- Ladies and gentlemen, I know you thought this was going to be a 747, but this DC-10 . . .
- Okay, make a U-turn. Then . . .
- You get used to that after you've lived here all your life.
- Here are your candles and matches.
- No, this is Saint Brunsmer in Belgium, not Holland.
- Sorry, everyone at the embassy is on vacation. Please leave name and hotel. This is a recording.
- They tore it down about three years ago.
- That's not our currency. We have no monkey on our hundred-dollar bill.
- That's what I tried telling you when you told me to shut up, Daddy. Maybe the gas station man found him.
- This is not your passport.
- Remember when I said I felt someone bump into me in that crowd back there? Well . . .
- The reason we act this way is because we *are* the only hotel in town.
- Is that a Jewish name?
- Cars don't backfire in short bursts.
- Honey, this is the fifth time he's driven past that statue.
- Honey, say something.
- Honey, are you going to let him talk to you that way?
- It does look like a bite of some kind.
- An American shot my father during the war.

- The doctor is cutting someone's hair at his shop right now.
- We do dance to God Bagzolla for you. He chase fever spirit.
- Of course it is still moving. It is alive.
- Wow, what a long hair.
- Take the next left. No, right. No, it's left.
- That's a map of Spain, not Italy.
- See if there are tar pits on the map.
- Look, a whole shelf of those rare vases we bought.
- You forgot to multiply by ten. That cost us $170, not $17.
- I'll be your guide all weekend. That is all English I know.
- No, the man you gave your bags to does not work here.
- When we took his cage off the plane, he looked like he was in a very deep sleep.
- These donkeys never make mistakes.
- Look, darling, that man running over there has an attaché case exactly like yours.
- He never bit anyone before.
- Wow, are you lost.
- Hey, Elmer, you'll never guess where these folks think they are!
- No, I don't remember you.
- What do you think—you were the first person to ever lose a wallet?
- Well, ladies and gentlemen, let's find out if one's first solo takeoff is the most exciting.
- Okay, here goes nothing!

▶ ▶ ▶ # Threatened in Spain

George Schultz is one of my most favorite human beings in the world. He's the owner of Pips, the first comedy club in America, and has been an invaluable help to my career. He is kind, hip, and hysterically funny, a great traveling companion.

However, this does not mean that when I am driving and lost I spare him any of my neurotic wrath. For example . . .

Somehow, on the single highway from Marbella to Málaga, Spain, I had gotten lost. George was one of three passengers who tried, under tremendous pressure, to read the map and help me, but I was beyond help. I had already reached the point where I was convinced that my being lost was a plot devised by a group of Nazis, in order to lure me into a trap where I would be tortured by the Gestapo.

By some miracle, I stumbled upon Málaga and even managed to park the car in a lot. Once my feet touched mother earth, I was becalmed, jovial, friendly, and concerned about the welfare and well-being of my friends. Now, to me, this makes up for any nastiness I may have exhibited when I was lost. However, some people, especially car mates of mine, would disagree.

Anyway, my lost fit aside, we had a splendid time in Málaga, enjoying the museums and sidewalk cafés. Unfortunately, we had arrived too late to see the ancient ruin and one museum, but whose fault was that? The Spanish road builders and mapmakers, of course.

When it came time to leave Málaga, George volunteered to drive us home. I was more than willing to do the driving, but everyone insisted that I had done enough for one day. (Actually, they said for the next six months.) So, George got behind the wheel, I sat next to him, and the two women got in the backseat. George pulled out of the parking lot. I rolled down my window to better see the sights I had missed on the way up, when I had been blinded by rage. Within moments, the two women were asleep.

When we hit the main highway, I thought I'd have some good-natured fun with George. The theme I decided on was "Instilling Self-doubt."

"George, when you're driving from Gibraltar to Marbella, should the Mediterranean be on your left or your right?"

"Right."

"You sure?"

"Positive."

I waited about five minutes before continuing.

"George, if you are driving from Málaga to Marbella, as you are actually doing right now, which side would the Mediterranean be on? Your right, or your left?"

"What are you being, a wiseass?"

"No. I just want to know which side the Med would be on from Málaga to Marbella."

"Where it is, schmucko, on your left."

"Then you're heading in the right direction, unless you're wrong about the Mediterranean. Then you'd be driving in the opposite direction you're supposed to be heading at . . . wow, at seventy-five miles an hour."

I had him! At least I thought I did, but remember I told you how hip George is? Well, with his eyes sharply focused on the road, his hands tightly gripping the wheel, he floored the accelerator and hissed at me.

"Listen, you neurotic bastard, I know exactly what you're trying to do. You want me to think I'm lost like you were today when you made nervous wrecks of all of us. Well, let me tell you something, you demented son of a bitch. One more word out of your conniving, cesspool mouth and I'll turn this car right into the oncoming traffic. I'll kill us all. I'm sorry the two young, Jewish lives in the backseat will be snuffed out in their prime, but I don't give a damn about myself. I'm sixty-two. I've lived. I've done it all. I've eaten Chinese food and I've come. So, go ahead, Charles Manson, let's hear one more word, one little peep. Try me!"

We were doing over ninety with our tires already over the median line. I said nothing for the next hour it took George to get us back to Marbella. I just sat there looking at the beautiful Mediterranean, which was on our left.

▼   ▼   ▼   # What's Your Sign?

No encouraging fighter pilots

Watch out for large black fingernail

Town of "Only" to the right

Two idiots playing up ahead

Caution: Christian drivers

Wanted: Sober arrow painter

No-passing-zone sign for idiots who don't understand symbols

Forks and knives for sale—no spoons

▼ ▼ ▼ **You'd Better Not**

Rub your chin in one country and absolutely nothing is thought of it, but in another country less than one hundred miles away, such a move is considered an insult to all members of one's family and they may kill you with impunity. If you were to cross your right leg over your left in public, no one anywhere would give it a thought, right? Wrong. There's a country where such an act is like saying the F-word to someone's mother and is punishable by solitary confinement in prison for no less than thirty years and a fine of forty thousand head of cattle.

As unbelievable as it may seem, such behaviors are the most important and most overlooked aspects of travel. Throughout my years of seeing the world, I have collected the "don'ts" of those places I've visited, and then some. I am happy to pass on to you those I feel are least likely to be found in any other travel book.

EUROPE (in general):

Don't make fun of their family names. Keep in mind that to an Eastern European, for example, the name Smith is funnier than their very common name Schmololinkinski.

If someone has a title, use it casually in conversation, such as "It is such a lovely day, Herr Brumskert, third heir to the now defunct Hapsburg Empire and first cousin to Baron Von Heshmeider, Prince of Bavaria and former Field Marshal of the SS, Nazi Son of a Bitch, so maybe a picnic on the lawn would be perfect."

When shaking hands with both males and females, outsqueeze the squeezer, stopping the pressure only when they yell, "Uncle and Aunt." Prior to entering a country, look up and memorize this expression in the native language so you will recognize it, not continuing to squeeze, which is considered a terrible social indiscretion.

One of the oldest superstitions in the world is that an entire nation will be cursed should a foreigner skip twice around a public fountain.

If you must skip, do so in your room or in the woods.

After sundown, do not wear your suit coat inside out.

AUSTRIA:

It is verboten to do the Kurt Waldheim goose step.

Don't stare in the direction of Germany with an expression of great fear.

BULGARIA:

This is a tough one to remember. A nod of the head means yes and shaking your head means no, so you'd better practice this before passing the street prostitutes.

If an old man asks you to pull his finger, don't do it.

Never bark back at a dog, for they believe this will make their women lose weight.

CZECHOSLOVAKIA:

If someone kicks a soccer ball through the window of the restaurant in which you are dining, kick it back.

Don't tell people that Czechoslovakia spoken backward is Aikavolsohcezc. It's an old joke and they hate it.

DENMARK:

Don't go into a sex-change clinic, whip it out, and ask how much it's worth as a trade-in.

On one of their topless beaches, don't wear flesh-toned saddlebags as a joke.

If you are a man and someone says he can fix you up with a tall blonde, remember that Danish men are also tall blonds, so you take it from there.

Don't tell a Dane that he is a great one.

Don't ask if they can change your whole spouse, instead of just his or her sex.

ENGLAND:

Don't throw a dead warthog at any member of the Royal Family.

If you happen to see the Royal Family, it is improper to try to get Princess Margaret's attention by blowing a dog whistle.

The English don't like to be referred to as "English," but as "British," so be certain to use the term "British" around the English, and not "English."

The British don't like to talk shop when drinking in the pubs. They prefer to get drunk, so be polite and get drunk. But don't get so tanked that you start to talk shop or call them "English."

The British don't like to hear rank jokes about the Royal Family, so jot the joke down on a piece of paper and hand it to them.

The British like to think they speak English, so don't correct them.

Don't mention how often, since the end of World War II, you have seen the sun set on the British Empire.

Don't complain about the weather. Remember, they think sunshine is wet.

Don't start an argument about chips being french fries.

They consider it impolite if you ask about their occupation, but they are very open about their sexual experiences with farm animals.

When someone toasts Her Majesty's health, don't add, "And let's hope they find Jimmy Hoffa," but you may drop your pants, especially if they are baggy, and make funny sounds with your mouth. They love that.

They know the white cliffs of Dover are a sickly off-off-gray, so don't comment on it.

FRANCE:

They don't like to speak English and they hate when someone brutalizes French, so when in France, don't say anything.

Don't tell them that they have proven many times over that twenty million Frenchmen *can* be wrong.

Don't ask to tour their fries factory.

Don't brag about the little French restaurant back in your hometown.

Don't remind them that most of the wine grapes in France came from California vineyards when most of theirs got wiped out.

Don't be seen drinking a bottle of Ripple or Thunderbird.

GERMANY:

Don't tell them you are there on business and your company constructs and repairs walls.

Don't show how worried you are about their reunification.

Don't ask them how their relatives who went to Argentina in 1945 are doing.

Don't ask them what their job was in the late thirties and early forties.

Don't comment about how the top industrial families of Hitler's Germany are now selling cars and kitchen equipment in the United States.

Don't ask if they are interested in trying to conquer the world for the third time.

Don't tell stories about a relative of yours who bombed them during World War II.

Don't invite their women to enter this year's Ernest Borgnine Look-alike Contest.

Don't ask them to name their famous comedians.

Don't speak Yiddish.

Don't laugh when they say they were only following orders.

Don't laugh.

GREECE:

Don't say how much you like Turkish taffy or Turkish coffee or Turkish anything.

Greeks generously give visitors things they say they like, so don't admire any farm animal you wouldn't want as a pet.

Don't say that you think their women should wear something other than black.

Don't hold your dirty handkerchief out for someone to hold when dancing. That's only in the movies.

Don't tell the joke about the Greek Orthodox priest and the camel.

Don't ask men if it's true about . . . you know.

Don't bend over. It is true.

IRELAND:

Don't keep your rental car if it backfires.

Here you can call the British "English," or anything you want.

Don't hang around with British soldiers.

When offered a drink, never say, "Thank you, but I don't drink."

When telling a story, don't tell it exactly as it happened.

They know President Kennedy was Irish, so don't start.

Don't ask what the hell the fighting is all about.

When asked which religion you are, say Buddhist.

Don't put a potato in your fly.

Don't pull a potato out of your fly.

Don't ask a woman if she is wearing an Erin Go Braugh.

Don't say North Carolina is greener.

If you don't know what to say, punch someone in the mouth.

Don't tell them that Saint Patrick's Day in Manhattan means beer cans and bottles all over the pavements and street and vomit all over everything else.

ISRAEL:

Don't keep your car if it backfires.

Don't pick up a rock.

Don't let anything be said without starting an argument over it. They love to argue: "You call this sunny?"

Do not accept anything without haggling over the price, because it's expected, but don't expect to outfox anyone.

Don't ask for a ham-and-cheese on white with butter and mayo and a glass of milk.

Don't ask why the fewer than 3 million Israelis are paranoid about the 100 million Arabs surrounding them who have sworn to push them into the sea.

Don't act shocked when you see Israelis and Arabs living together and getting along perfectly well outside the West Bank.

Don't tell them about all your Jewish friends back home.

Don't recite your bar mitzvah prayer and speech.

If you are Jewish, don't feel or act guilty about not living there. If you are Christian, you can feel guilty.

Don't ask if the wall ever answers.

Don't lie about Golda Meir's looks. They know.

If you are Jewish, don't ask to see the trees your family planted.

Don't buy dirt from the Mound and remember the camera wasn't invented at the time of the Last Supper.

If you have an Arab guide, at sundown don't say, "Mecca, schmecca, let's get back to the Sheraton."

ITALY:

Don't ask if it is true that when a man stares too long at the Leaning Tower of Pisa, he becomes impotent.

Don't remind them that the Chinese created spaghetti and Marco Polo brought it back to Italy.

If the Pope is blessing the throng in St. Peter's Square, it is in bad taste to scream out "Bingo!"

It is insulting not to join in on all arguments over traffic accidents. If you don't speak Italian, simply wave your hands around like a bird about to take off and continuously yell the word "Fongu!"

NETHERLANDS:

Don't ask if their wooden shoes are warp-proof.
Don't ask if some wooden shoes come with wooden shoelaces.
Don't do dike jokes.
They really don't care if you love tulips. However, it is in bad taste to eat a tulip in public.

NORWAY:

During the summer months, it is impolite to ask, "When the hell is the sun going to set?"
Don't ask them what they've been doing since they stopped being Vikings.
Don't overstate how much you like their salmon. And don't ask if they know it is called "belly lox" in the USA.
It is rude to mention that no Norwegian has ever played in a World Series.

POLAND:

They love Norwegian jokes, especially the one about how it takes one Norwegian to change a light bulb.
If you borrow the library book, don't forget to return it.
If you are stupid enough to tell a Polish joke, don't forget to speak very slowly and wait a long time after the punch line.
Print words very large.
Don't tell them that the Rubik's Cube puzzles that were sold *outside* Poland were not blue on all six sides.
Don't stare or laugh at the three men changing a light bulb.
Don't criticize the painting they have hanging in their museum.
It is a very serious offense to forge someone's "X" on a check.

SCOTLAND:

Don't put mirrors on the tips of their shoes.

It is considered highly rude to swim naked on your back and yell, "Look, the Loch Ness Monster!"

No one cares that your son's name is Scott.

You'd better get this one straight: Scotch is a liquor. People living in Scotland are Scots or Scotsmen. The tape is not Scots tape or Scotsmen tape. It is Scotch tape. Scottish is of Scotland. Scot itch is when your kilt is made of rough wool. Scotch is not your son's name. Scott is, and still, no one gives a damn.

It is disrespectful to say you don't hear the melodic quality of a bagpipe, so just sit there and make believe you adore the sounds created by squeezing air out of a dead pig's stomach.

Don't borrow money, but if it is absolutely necessary, after you are handed the money, immediately hand it back. Interest should be discussed beforehand.

Don't ask if it is true that when a chameleon wanders onto a plaid kilt, it will explode.

SPAIN:

They've had it up to here with requests for the nonexistent fly.

Don't take chrysanthemums to someone's house when invited to dinner, for the flower represents death, unless, of course, you know for certain that during dinner someone will pass away.

If you attend a funeral, bring chrysanthemums, but don't eat, not even a nosh.

If you are tossed the bull's ear after the kill, thank the matador, put the ear in your pocket, and wait until you are back in your hotel room to throw up.

The story about the small and large meatballs is a myth, but don't eat the dark sausages.

It is tasteless to laugh at or yell "encore" to a one-legged flamenco dancer.

Remember that Spain is about as happy with Christopher Columbus as are the American Indians. How they blew being the number-one power in the world is a touchy subject. Also, no one wants to hear how hard Spanish 101 was. Just remember that "chicken and rice" is not "arrows can polo."

No one really gives a flying you-know-what about how many street signs in America are written in Spanish.

Keep in mind, before you criticize, that they have as much trouble understanding why American men like to shoot little rabbits with big guns as Americans do trying to comprehend why they kill bulls.

SWEDEN:

You can stare, but it is impolite to drool when you look at their women.

Don't tell people you think you are going crazy because you keep thinking you are seeing people who have been in Ingmar Bergman's movies, because you *are* seeing people who were in his films.

Because Sweden is the suicide capital of the world, don't say anything upsetting that might motivate someone to take their life, such as "The bus seems to be a couple minutes late" or "It looks like it might drizzle."

When meeting a woman or man, don't ask them to prove it.

Drunken driving is a very serious offense, and sometimes a policeman is sober enough to catch you.

It is bad taste to spread the word that you are available to act in an adult film.

SWITZERLAND:

Think of something else to discuss besides cuckoo clocks, watches, chocolate, neutrality, skiing, and banking, such as . . . eh . . . like . . . eh . . .

Whatever you do, don't yodel.

Don't ask where the drug kingpins hang out after depositing their laundered money.

Don't ask a banker how many ex-Nazis he sees in any given month.

Don't keep repeating "It looks just like a postcard."

In public, it is considered vulgar to eat a Hershey bar.

They never heard of the Family Robinson, and the few who have don't want to hear about them anymore.

TURKEY:

Don't argue. Just buy a carpet. Trust me.

Don't tell anyone if your name is Spiros or Napoleon.

Remember, you never saw or heard of the movie *Midnight Express*. However, if you are sent to a prison, it is perfectly okay to nail the back of your pants to your cell wall.

Don't make a fool of yourself by asking for Turkish cigarettes. All their cigarettes are Turkish.

USSR:

Don't bring into the country any book that could be labeled "dissident literature," such as *Bambi*, which is symbolic of the revolutionaries imprisoned by the Czar who later on spied for him. Get it?

Now, I'm going to give you a word to forget while you are in Russia, and the word is *Russia*. You are in the Soviet Union.

If you see anyone speaking to a dead person, pay no attention, because no one in the Soviet Union is dead until the government says they are dead.

In the overall scheme of life, it really doesn't matter who invented television, the automobile, or the Hula-Hoop, so let them take credit for it.

Gorbachev has nothing on his head—no mark, nothing!

Don't say that Afghanistan was their Vietnam, because they will retort that Vietnam was your Afghanistan, which makes about as much sense.

Don't offer to buy a cup of coffee for the man who has been following you everywhere.

Don't complain after standing in a movie line for two hours only to discover you've been waiting to purchase toilet paper.

In Chernobyl, it is rude to call anyone "four eyes," even if they *are* wearing glasses.

Take photos only of clouds, but be certain there isn't a plane flying near them.

No matter how tempting, do not join in the game "Refuseniks."

Don't tell anyone you believe it is cruel to kill animals for their fur, unless you are prepared to spend the winter wrapped around some party official's neck.

If someone offers you five million rubles for your hat, refuse, because there is nothing you can buy in Siberia.

Don't act frightened when you see the eye in the center of a flower on your wallpaper, even when it blinks. Same applies to sneezes coming out of your night lamp.

If an old man offers you his finger, pull it.

YUGOSLAVIA:

They hate rumors, so don't tell them Tito is dead.

Don't say, "I had no idea your country was so beautiful." It is not their fault they are being handled by a bad public relations firm.

Remember that their favorite American pop singer is Merv Griffin.

If anyone looks at your hair, says, "Dello bas guvnick," and then laughs, laugh along with them. To them this is very funny.

Don't ever say in a crowd, "Is it me, or is the ground shaking?"

▼ ▼ ▼ **What's Your Sign?**

 Lego-people beds for sale

 Coffins for sale ahead

 Did you write home?

 Fish crossing

 Welcome to Japan

A schmuck lives up ahead

Start here for Italian tour

▲ ▲ ▲ **Wax Johnson**

In 1986, when my son, Cole, was four and a half years old, I took him to Croix Val Mer, a small coastal town along the French Riviera, where I had rented a house for two weeks. There was plenty for a little boy to do, including a swimming pool at the house, the nearby beach, an amusement park, and plenty of toys and games. But one day when Cole seemed restless and I was in a little zanier mood than usual, I concocted a wonderful story for a wonderful little boy.

We took a ride to St.-Tropez. I pointed to what looked like a castle atop a high hill overlooking the town.

"The tallest Jewish giant in the world lives there. His name is Wax."

"I heard about him."

Now how could my son have heard about someone who didn't even exist until I made him up thirty seconds ago?

"Oh, you have? What's his last name?"

"Johnson," Cole answered without any hesitation.

"Right. You do know him, but did you know about some of the brave things he's done for France and her people?"

Cole admitted that he only knew about a few, so I proceeded to spin intricate and colorful webs of courageous exploits. When I was finished, Cole's curiosity was piqued and he wanted to visit Wax Johnson. I knew he would. It was part of my plan.

Early that evening, we bought a large loaf of bread, an entire block of cheese, and a gallon jug of wine and put it in a basket. We placed this in the trunk of our car and headed for St.-Tropez and Wax Johnson's castle.

Cole's main concern was that there wasn't enough food for someone who stood six stories high and weighed 23,408 pounds in his stocking feet (which were a size 142, triple Z). I assured him that it was only a token snack and Wax would be very happy to receive it. Next time, I'd ask the baker if he could make a bagel the size of a truck tire.

Even up close, the Nautical Museum looked like a castle in which a giant would live. I found an opening in the Cyclone fence and Cole and I slipped through it. We climbed to a point where we could see one side of the castle clearly. We whispered and moved cautiously, Cole because of Wax Johnson, and I because of museum guards. We lay on a grassy knoll and looked up at the castle. We didn't speak for a few minutes. I knew Cole's little heart was beating like crazy. Remembering how vivid and wild my imagination was at his age, and how I would succumb to the power of adult suggestion, I suddenly pointed to the largest window, from which shone a yellow light.

"Look, Cole. That window. Wax Johnson's eye!"

Of course, Cole saw it, too. He even remarked how only the pupil showed.

"Let's wave to let him know we're here."

We waved. The eye disappeared and we made our way back to our car. We each held a handle of the picnic basket and placed it down in front of the main gate of the museum, which I knew would be locked in the evening.

I rang a fake bell and got on a fake intercom, into which I spoke a fake French, asking a fake housekeeper to please tell Wax Johnson that Cole Jay Brenner came by to say hello and left a little snack for him of his favorite wine and cheese. Cole was literally squirming with excitement.

We drove into St.-Tropez for dinner. At the restaurant, I secretly asked the waiter to come to my table in a few minutes and tell me that Wax Johnson was on the phone for me. When he did it, Cole's eyes almost bulged out of his head and he applauded. I left the table and went upstairs to the phone. When I returned, Cole asked me what Wax Johnson had said. With enough volume to awaken the dead buried in St.-Tropez, and definitely loud enough to startle the other diners, I imitated a giant's voice, yelling:

"Thank Cole for the snack!"

It was the most excited I had ever seen my son. He could hardly eat his dinner. On the way home, Cole asked me to drive by Wax's castle to see if he really ate the food. I figured that someone must have discovered and removed the basket by then, so I did. The food was gone. Cole was thrilled. So was I.

All Cole could talk about the next day was Wax Johnson and what had happened. While Cole was swimming in the pool, I sat on the terrace and dialed random phone numbers, writing down the numbers I chose. Finally, I found what I was looking for: a long recording in French.

I printed a note to Cole from Wax Johnson, thanking him for the bread, cheese, and wine, and saying how much he regretted not being able to come out when he saw us wave to him. He asked Cole to call him later that evening and left his phone number. I placed it on the front step where I knew Cole would find it when we left the house to go to dinner. When we did, I walked right over the note. Cole spotted it. He handed it to me and I read it to him. He freaked out.

After dinner and a short walk along the marina to see the boats, we returned to the house. Of course, Cole wanted to make his call immediately. I forewarned Cole that, although Wax Johnson understood and wrote perfectly in English, he spoke only French. I watched Cole dial the number. When the recording came on, Cole beamed and spoke a few words timidly, saying who he was and how happy he was about Wax's enjoying his snack. When the recording finally stopped repeating and the dial tone came on, Cole hung up.

"What did Wax Johnson say to you, Cole, if you don't mind my asking?"

"I'm not sure of everything, Dad, but I think he thanked me again for the food and asked me to come see him."

You can drive to a closed museum only so many times before a child becomes suspicious, or more importantly, disappointed. So, on the second visit, I once again got on the fake intercom and received a message for Cole.

"Cole, Wax Johnson isn't home, but he left a message for you. A big bridge on the Seine River in Paris was badly damaged last night by a storm. It could collapse any moment. Wax Johnson went there right away to stand in the water and hold the bridge up so they can repair it. Once again, he has saved the lives of many people. He said to tell you that he might not return before we leave, but to make sure that the next time you are in France, you call him."

Cole didn't say anything. I was so worried that I had innocently set him up for a hurt, and the whole thing had backfired. Finally, Cole took my hand and began walking down the path toward our car.

"Dad?"

"Yes, Cole."

"Wax Johnson is a very brave giant, isn't he?"

"The bravest Jewish giant in the whole world."

"The biggest one, too, right, Dad?"

"Yes"—I laughed—"and the biggest."

"Are we coming back to France soon?"

"Maybe next summer."

"Good. I'll see Wax Johnson then. Can I have an ice cream, Dad?"

"Of course. Wow, Cole, can you imagine how big the cone has to be for Wax Johnson's ice cream? I'll bet . . ."

The first day Cole walked into his room in my house in New York, Wax Johnson's note was framed and on his night table. Over the following months, Cole looked at it often and spoke about his giant friend with a lot of love.

For one month the following summer, I rented a villa for my family and friends in the hills of St.-Tropez, a stone's throw from Wax Johnson's castle.

Cole was very anxious to see his giant friend, but he wanted to share the experience with his best and oldest friend, Zachary, my manager's son, who is three months older than Cole. I thought it was a magnanimous gesture on the part of a five-and-a-half-year-old child, so I agreed that he wait.

The day after Zack arrived, we packed the usual lunch for Wax Johnson and drove to the castle. I had checked that it would be closed that day. This time I borrowed my father's videotape recorder to capture the event for posterity.

The huge pothole outside the main gate was perfect for a giant's footprint. When Cole and Zack stood in it, they babbled away about how big Wax Johnson's shoe must be. The old intercom was still not there, so I got on it and announced that Cole Brenner was back in France and he and his best friend, Zachary Reidman, wanted to come in for a chat.

This time the message left for Cole was that Wax Johnson had to help rescue a disabled French battleship. It asked Cole to forgive him for not being there, but he extended an invitation to Cole to see his house anytime he wanted that week.

The invitation to see the castle tempered the disappointment of Wax's not being there. We left the food at the gate and followed a footpath that wrapped around the museum. Cole pointed out the window where he had seen Wax Johnson's eye. Zack was skeptical about the eye. As a matter of fact, he distrusted the whole story of Wax Johnson. Zack had always been a serious realist and Cole an imaginative dreamer. That's why the story worked with one and not the other. I knew that I had to do something to at least put a plausible doubt in Zack's mind, to prevent him from breaking Cole's bubble and maybe even his heart.

In a treetop a short distance down the path, I saw a big black bird. It gave me an idea.

"Oh, boys, I almost forgot to mention that Wax Johnson said that when the snack you left was taken into the castle this time, the housekeeper will release Wax Johnson's black raven, which is to fly over us to let us know the food is safely inside."

I was counting on the bird's taking flight as we approached his tree, especially with the added help of a stone I held in my hand. Just as anticipated, as we got closer, without a stone's being thrown, the bird spread its wings and flew directly overhead. Cole screamed and jumped up in the air. Zack's face was puzzled. Perfect. The seed of doubt had been planted, the Wax Johnson story saved.

Because I knew that Zack would never believe any of the stories I would be concocting during our tour of the castle, I took Cole on a day that Zack went for a ride with his father.

Inside the museum, I spun the wildest stories. The huge anchor was Wax Johnson's watch fob, the tall ship's mast was his toothpick, the ship's bell was rung to announce dinner, and all the ship models were ships rescued by Wax Johnson throughout the years. For every object, I had a story, and for every story, I had a mesmerized and delighted son. When we were leaving, I told the guard in English to please thank Wax Johnson for allowing us in his castle, to say how much we loved it, and that Cole hoped he was well—and best of luck with the battleship. The guard had no idea what the hell I was talking about, but Cole did, and that was all that mattered.

That evening, Cole told his doubting Thomas friend everything he saw. A few days later, he shared the letter he received from Wax Johnson with Zack, who, of course, didn't buy one word of any of it.

Today, the two Wax Johnson letters sit side by side in Cole's bookcase, and every once in a while, he speaks to me about him. I hope that Cole never stops believing in his giant friend and that, no matter how much a realist he may become as he matures, he always leaves room inside himself for delightful imagination.

Long live Wax Johnson!

★ ★ ★ # Honoring the Competition

I'd be an egomaniac to think I had written the ultimate travel guide, eliminating the need for all other printed sources of travel information. Although you must admit that this book is among the top five on the subject, right? Thank you. Anyway, always a believer in fair play, I submit a list of competitive travel guides that I personally recommend. I know you will find them as useful for your travels at home and abroad as I.

ALASKA: Expensive Gasoline but Free Oil

BUFFALO: Where You Got It Made if You're a Snowman Who Can Bowl

CALCUTTA, INDIA: We Fast and We Bad

CALIFORNIA: Where It's Not Our Fault if You Live on One

CHICAGO: Voted Best Place to Visit and That Was Just by the Dead Ones

DENMARK: Where Men Are Men, Women Are Men, Men Are Women, Women Like to Dress as Men, Men Like to Dress as Women, Women . . .

GERMANY: Service with a Heil

IRELAND: On Six Quarts a Day

INTERCOURSE, PENNSYLVANIA: Visit, Then Leave, Then Visit, Then Leave, Then Visit, Then Leave, Then Visit, Then Leave . . .

JERUSALEM: What, Am I Talking to a Wall?

INSIDE NEW YORK: What the Hell Youse Lookin' At? Youse Never Seen No Travel Guide Before, or What?

NEWARK: Gateway to New Jersey

SECAUCUS: Gateway to Newark

SOUTH PHILLY: Yo! Frankie Avalon Lived over Dere, Mario Lanza's Stoop's Dere, Wilt Chamberlain Dunked Dere, Dave Brenner He Grew Up Dere, Cosby Went ta Dat School Dere, Dick Clark's Dancers Danced Dere, and Whatta Yize Lookin' At?

SAN FRANCISCO: Where It's Only a Drag if You Want It to Be

THE TENNESSEE HILLS: One Big, Happy Family, Literally

POLAND: Where . . . Eh . . .

VISIT TAIWAN: Where the Stamp "Made in Taiwan" Is Made

GREENLAND: Where the Nights Are Long and the Nights Are Long

COME TO THE NORTH POLE: Find Out Why You Never Got That Train Set You Wanted

RENO: Where, When the Going Gets Ugly . . .

GREECE: Without Bending Your Budget—Or Over

VISIT NORTH DAKOTA: No One Else Does

THE HIMALAYAS: Let Our Asses Take Yours Up

Don't Bang Your Head Against the Wall for Where to Go—BANG-KOK

HAITI: Birthplace of Haitians

VIRGIN ISLANDS: Yeah, Sure

Go Dutch in HOLLAND

POLAND: The Only Country Whose Name Is Spelled the Same Forward and Backward

LIVERPOOL: Not Easy to Swim in It but It's Good for You

MANILA: Home of the Envelope

BEIRUT: Visit Your Hostages

ISRAEL: You Don't Write and You Don't Call so the Least You Can Do Is Visit

BHUTAN: The Only Country That Means "Whore" in Italian

VISIT LIECHTENSTEIN: If You Can Find Us

ISRAEL: Even a Postcard Would Be Nice

CONGO: We Hate to Beat Our Own Drum, But . . .

COOK ISLAND: Anyone Can Learn

DJIBOUTI: We Have Too Many Tourists as It Is

ISRAEL: Just Wait Until You Have Your Own Country and No One Comes to Visit, Then You'll Know

BURKINA: We Just Heard of Ourselves, Too

LESOTHO: The Only Country Named by an Explorer with a Lisp

MALDIVES: We Only Sound like a Skin Rash

Promise Her Anything but Give Her SWAZILAND

SEYCHELLES: If You Hold Us Up to Your Ear You'll Hear Billy Ocean

THAILAND: We Also Sell Belts and Shirts

TOGO: Or Not to Go

TRINIDAD AND TOBAGO: Once Upon a Time, Two Brothers Named . . .

TUVALU: Learn to Play the Balotempol and Eat Sincasooka

ISRAEL: Sure, Go to Tuvalu Before Coming By Us. We Won't Lose Any Sleep over It, Believe Me

There's Your Way, the Right Way, and ZIMBABWE

ZAMBIA: Hello. Is Anyone Here?

SHANGRI-LA: Don't We Wish

UTOPIA: You Tell Us Where We Are

More Things You Hate to Hear

- Still glad we took the scenic back roads?
- No, *you* ask.
- It looks like it stopped bleeding. Okay, according to page nineteen, under "Colloquialisms," you told him, "Even a dead pig is better looking than your mother." Oh! It started bleeding again.
- You're the one who took a year of Spanish in high school.
- You're the first tourist we've seen in ten years.
- I *swear* the guide said the bus would wait here.
- It is rare that the bridge gets washed away.
- American troops destroyed this village, wounding 813, killing 242, including my two brothers.
- Let's see. It reads, "Water . . . contaminated." Why?
- You have no choice.
- How was I to know it was a gay dance hall?
- How was I to know it was a straight dance hall?
- It's every man for himself!
- He did warn us that one more word and he'd leave us out here.
- The State Department declared this country *what?*
- They took another hostage here today.
- Having fun?
- Are we having fun yet?
- In your country, I believe they call it poison ivy.
- They have to clear some wreckage off the runway.
- Make room at the rail—quick!
- Of course I can hear the boiler room over the phone. Now how may I help you, sir?
- You'll have to share your cabin.
- They are flying in the part by helicopter.
- I'm certain they heard our SOS.
- It's just an optical illusion that we're going to collide. However . . .
- The outboard motor is supposed to be tied to the dinghy just so something like that doesn't happen.
- No one has a match?
- My feet are getting wet.
- My waist is getting wet.
- My *blub blub blub blub blub* . . .

- Did you see how drunk the captain got at dinner?
- "Singles" includes anyone without a mate, regardless of age.
- Your seat is right in front of the fire-eater.
- At least three out of four passengers have already gotten it.
- We're from Schenectady. Where you from?
- Hi. I'm Ted Tillman, and this here is the little woman, Gertrude. Been wearing the ball and chain forty-seven years. Ha-ha. Only joking. Say, did you hear the one about the one-eyed . . .
- Here's our home address and phone number. Give us yours.

★ ★ ★ Pleeze, Mistah

I know that I join most people in the belief that everyone on earth has the right to pursue an honest living, and I am as empathetic with the poor and needy as the next guy. However, every passing year, I am finding it more and more annoying when on a vacation not to be able to walk down a street, cross a lobby, sit in a restaurant, or lie on a beach without someone's trying to sell me something I wouldn't want in a million years. I hate shielding my eyes from the sun as I sit up on the beach to tell a vendor I don't want a straw hat with bells on it, or politely break away from someone on the street by telling them I already have a donkey puppet at home. I hate rushing for the hotel elevator to avoid having to wave away nicely a man who has a sparkling spider crawling across his head.

After years of trying to cope with this problem, I think I have found the solution. It works almost every time. Right before the vendors begin their pitch, I begin mine. That is, I try to sell them something—anything—that I have: my beach mat, comb, pocket fuzz, fork and spoon, anything.

Only once did someone top me. He actually gave me his whistling yo-yo for my Greek worry beads. I think I won because I have since kept the yo-yo with me to sell when I travel.

◆   ◆   ◆   # Lower the Drawbridge

My much older brother, Moby, and I finally took a trip we had always talked about. We referred to it as "the brothers' trip." We spent a few exciting days in London and then took a motor tour of the resplendent British countryside. It was a great decision. Every mile of every day, beauty and wonders bombarded us.

One afternoon, from the top of a sun-splashed grassy hill, we saw it in the valley below: the ruins of an ancient castle.

When I was a child, my brother filled my young mind with extraordinary images of Tarzan swinging through the African jungle, Sherlock Holmes solving another unsolvable crime, King Arthur and the Knights of the Round Table, swashbucklers like Captain Blood and Bluebeard, the Hunchback ringing the bells of Notre Dame, and his childhood favorite, the origin of his nickname— Moby Dick. Yes, along with my mother, my brother had nurtured my love of books. I read addictively, and my little world grew.

Now, there we stood. Teacher and student. Man and man. Brother and brother. Sir Moby and Sir David, heroic knights of King Arthur's court. Always ready, able, and willing to do battle.

Without an exchange of one word, with a mere glimpse at the glint in each other's eyes, my brother and I knew the job that had to be done. We drew our imaginary broadswords from their sheaths, and with our sturdy invisible mounts below, we charged down the hill, screaming cries of attack, toward the castle of our enemies.

We rode across the small gully to the moat, overgrown with centuries of grass, across the long-gone drawbridge, past where impregnable gates once stood, into the very courtyard of the castle. We fought the ghosts of the past from atop our trusty steeds until they died of their wounds. Then, on foot, we chopped off heads and pierced hearts. Boldly, we leapt onto the remains of the steps that lead up to the cell wherein was imprisoned the fair maiden, King Arthur's lady, Guinevere. Faster and more deadly than the Black Knight and Sir Lancelot, we slew all who stood in our way, until at last, we stood on the remains of the second floor. The two guards at the cell door were easily handled by Sir Moby's knife, and we burst into the cell and freed the fair maiden, who, thank goodness, was still fair. Shielding her from attacking throngs, we battled our way back down the stairs.

It was at the very instant that we were dealing with the last dozen or so swordsmen, in quick and efficient fashion I might add, that enemy replacements arrived.

There were about sixty of them. They were dressed strangely in what would someday be called "shirts, slacks, jumpsuits, jogging outfits, shorts, and sneakers." They were the knights and damsels of the Twentieth Century Order of the Tour Bus, a most deadly group.

Sir Moby and I decided to spare their lives, but not to allow them to interfere with our storybook rescue, so we continued killing off the knights who stood in our way. Sir Moby beheaded an archer, who was about to let fly an arrow into my heart, with one mighty swing of a sword he had pulled out of the chest of a dead man. When all were dead, we each kissed the hand of our Lady and escaped on foot, past the gaping Tourists of the Long Bus, out of the castle, through the tall grass to a spot on top of the hill from whence we came. There, we collapsed in gales of laughter, which I attributed in part to the strains of battle, but mostly to our family credo:

Sometimes you have to allow your imagination to go wild and be free enough not to give a damn what anyone thinks.

▶ ▶ ▶ **Four One-
Dollar Bills**

The Egyptian tour guide aboard our Nile cruise ship gave us a choice of riding a minibus to the temple or taking an early-morning walk through the fields. I always prefer walking to riding, especially in foreign countries. You see so much more and get a better feel for the life of the people.

He gave me explicit instructions for how to get there. It was very simple: I merely had to climb up a small embankment, the only embankment, and follow the dirt road in front of it, the only dirt road. My kind of directions.

At the top of the embankment, the road was there, exactly as he had described. After ten minutes or so of walking leisurely, I had a "feeling," which is the only way I can describe it, that I was not on the correct road. Ridiculous, right? The Egyptologist had been bringing tours here for the past twelve years. He had pointed to the only embankment, which I had climbed, and I was walking along the only dirt road there, so how could it possibly be wrong? It couldn't, but I knew for some inexplicable reason that it *was.*

Playing nearby were four Egyptian children, three boys and a girl, ranging in age from six to ten. The girl was already a dark beauty with sparkling black eyes and an ingratiating smile. I approached them. The girl explained with her rather limited English vocabulary that the two smaller boys were her brothers and the oldest boy, if I was interpreting her facial expression and tone correctly, wasn't to be trusted.

With words and gestures, I was able to ask if this was the road to the ancient temple. They simultaneously shook their heads and pointed to a nearby field. They volunteered to take me through the tall grass to what I assumed was the right road. I signaled for them to lead the way.

As we walked along together, they were having a grand time laughing at and with the giant stranger. When we came out of the field, we were standing on another dirt road identical to the one I had been on. They pointed up the road toward what I assumed would be the temple. I reached into my pocket and handed each one a folded U.S. one-dollar bill. The three youngest excitedly babbled some kind of thanks; the little girl added a big hug. She was so adorable and so right about the oldest boy. He tagged along with me pleading for more money, trying to convince me that the others had somehow stolen his share. He was no way as convincing a hustler as I was at his age. I indicated clearly that I wasn't buying it, and he left to run back to the others.

Twenty-five minutes later, I stood in front of the entrance to the temple. The guide ran up to me and told me how happy he was to see me, and he apologized. It seems that this was the first time the cruise ship had not docked in its usual spot. There was no way he could tell the difference; the embankment was identical, and coincidentally had an identical dirt road at the top of it. Only when he was on the minibus did he realize it. He asked me how I managed to find the right road. I smiled and shrugged.

I didn't know how to explain it. I still don't. I don't believe in anything supernatural. But how do you explain how I instinctively knew I was lost, and why, before leaving my cabin that morning, I had folded four dollar bills—U.S. currency, which I had not needed or used since arriving in Egypt—and put them in a separate pocket?

▼ ▼ ▼ You'd Better Not

I discussed specific customs in various countries in Europe earlier; now let's bounce around the rest of the world for a bit.

ARGENTINA:

It is impolite to begin a dinner conversation with, "So, what's been happening in the Falklands lately?" or "So, have all the Nazis you took in after the Second World War managed to assimilate?" or "So, when you were hiding Dr. Mengele here, did any of you personally spend any time with him?" or "So, can you believe some Broadway producer actually came up with an idea of a musical based on a woman who was a hooker, became a dictator's lover, spent millions on herself while her countrymen lived in poverty, and helped smuggle Nazi war criminals into her country?"

If you want to really make a good impression, say you love to eat wheat, maize, potatoes, sorghum, sugar, grapes, apples, citrus fruit, soybeans, beef, sunflower seeds, cotton, sheep, fish, lumber, coal, oil, natural gas, uranium, iron ore, lead, and zinc, because these are their main exports.

Don't get off the plane wearing a riding outfit and yell, "I'm ready for the pampas, but is the pampas ready for me?"

AUSTRALIA:

They hate hearing "Would somebody like another shrimp on the barbie?"

When they brag about Queensland's being "the Sunshine State," don't remind them that it also has the world's highest incidence of skin cancer.

They really don't want to show you a kangaroo or a wallaby, any more than you want to run around with some foreign tourist looking for a bald eagle and a buffalo.

Remember when swimming that the odds of being attacked by a shark are more than 10,000,000 to 1, but also keep in mind that the odds against growing back a leg are much, much greater.

CANADA:

It is considered in bad taste, as well as stupid, to ask a Royal Mounted policeman if he got his man.

Don't compliment anyone on how well they speak English. This also applies to people in Montreal, but for a different reason.

Don't tell people in Nova Scotia you came there for lox.

Don't look up at the sky and say, "Looks like acid rain."

CHINA:

Don't ask people, "Are my shirts ready?"

Don't say to anyone, "Didn't you just walk around the corner back there?"

Don't scream, "Wow, I've never seen so many people in my life!"

Don't paint "Zito 125th Street" on the Great Wall.

Don't ask if Lenny Bruce's idea is correct, that they decide the names of their children by dropping silverware on the floor.

Don't wait on a corner for a cab longer than six days.

Don't ask for the other menu—the one with Column A and Column B.

Don't call anyone "number-one son."

Don't get upset when they think you, your spouse, and your neighbor are triplets.

CUBA:

Do not refer to the women swimming at the beach as "the Bay of Pigs."

Don't lie to them and say that all the demented prisoners Castro conned President Carter into accepting have all adjusted quite well and are credits to the communities in which they settled, especially South Miami.

Don't question whether Fidel sleeps with his beard over or under the covers.

If Fidel asks to pull your finger, let him.

EGYPT:

Don't complain how noisy Cairo is, because the noise problem doesn't bother them, and besides, they probably won't be able to hear you anyway.

Never hand anyone a gift with your left hand, unless, of course, the gift is your right hand.

Don't do hieroglyphic jokes, such as, "Hello. My name is two birds, a scepter, three squiggly lines, and one eye."

JAPAN:

Never address anyone by their first name, unless, of course, their name is Yakatoro Yakatoro.

When bowing in greeting, don't turn it into a Groucho Marx impression.

When eating dinner, don't stand a mushroom up on the table, shield your eyes, and imitate atomic-bomb sounds and scream.

Don't be rude and remind them that we won the war, or they may be rude in return and remind you that they won the peace.

Don't ask for free tickets to Radio City.

Don't ask if it's true that they put a down payment on the White House.

Never point to the top of a tall building in Tokyo and yell, "Godzilla! Run for your lives!"

LIBYA:

Don't ask people, "Where's Zipper Brain's palace?"
When you find the Royal Palace of Qaddafi, don't pose for a picture in front of it, spinning your index finger in a circle next to your temple.

MEXICO:

Don't suggest to a cabdriver that his field of vision would improve greatly if he were to remove the velvet balls that are hanging all around the inside.
It is uncouth to request that your enchiladas be made with Swiss cheese.
Don't ask for the closest Taco Bell.

PHILIPPINES:

Don't ask people if they really believe she bought that many shoes.
Don't bounce a rubber ball on the pavement while reciting, "P, my name is Phyllis, my mother's name is Paula, we come from the Philippines where we sell phobias."
If you have sex with a native, don't tell your partner, "You are the thrilla in Manila!"

U.S.A.:

Don't tell an American he is not living in the only country in the world and that forms of government other than democracy work great in some countries.

They know that almost every President they have had was a schmuck, but they don't like foreigners, even ones who are now citizens, to say it.

Americans are emotionally vocal promoters of individual freedom and human rights in other countries, so don't remind them about their blacks, Hispanics, Indians, Haitians, women, the poor, and the elderly.

Don't call the police if you see people wearing weird clothing and matching colored wigs and whose faces are painted strange colors. They are not escapees from a mental hospital, but are sports fans on the way to a game.

The best way of knowing what not to do is to use *all* the aforementioned advice, because the U.S.A. is made up of people from every country listed, and some of the "old country" is still in them—except for the Indians, who have been living in their "old country" all this time. But don't remind the "Americans" of this.

RETURNING HOME

▲ ▲ ▲ ▲ ▲ ▲ ▲ ▲ ▲ ▲ ▲

Hi, Operator

The plane arrived three hours late. There was a delay getting the baggage. It was pouring outside and I had to wait nearly an hour for a cab. There was an accident on the road, tying us up for about thirty minutes. I dozed during the rest of the trip.

I was too tired to unpack, so I tossed my bag on the floor near the bathroom, undressed quickly, and climbed into the bed. My back was bothering me. It had been bad for most of these five weeks I had been on the road, the last two weeks of which were one-nighters, a different city in a different state every night for fourteen straight nights. I picked up the phone and dialed the operator.

"Hi, operator. Could I please have a wake-up call at eight?"

"Excuse me, sir?"

"A wake-up at eight."

"I don't understand, sir."

"Is this the operator?"

"Yes, sir."

"Well, then could you call me at eight tomorrow morning— actually, this morning—to wake me up?"

"We don't provide that service, sir."

"Come on, operator, are you telling me that this is the only hotel in America that has no wake-up service?"

"Sir, I am a New York City telephone operator. I'm sure, if you hang up and redial your hotel operator, she will be glad to give you a wake-up call."

"Operator, I just realized something. I'm not in a hotel. Thank you, operator, and good night."

"Good night, sir."

I hung up and was asleep before my head hit my very own pillow in my very own bed in my very own home. Sometimes the road can be a bitch.

▼ ▼ ▼ **What's Your Sign?**

 No Rolls-Royces

 Leaving town of "Only"

 First letter of alphabet has to be repeated

Man selling boxes up ahead

Right-side arrow painter drunk

Don't do nuthin'

Truck stuck on wedge of cheese up ahead

Stop arguing

◇   ◇   ◇   # Who, What, Where, When, & Why?

The following are questions you would ask *only* when traveling:

Is it after it simmers that you baste the dog in its own juices?
Did you know that in my country boiled eyes are not a delicacy?
Why did you wait until my last bite to tell me they were flambéed goat genitals?
Doesn't it hurt the mule when you cut those off?
You really never heard of the ASPCA?
Did you ever consider changing the name of your country to "Diarrhea"?

▼

Is it an FAA regulation that coffee must be served ten seconds before rough turbulence?
If it isn't my child sitting next to me, do I still have to put an oxygen mask over their face?

Driver, are you sure there is a twenty-percent tax for all American taxi passengers wearing blue?
In your brochure, why didn't you mention that your quaint hotel is right next door to a meat-packing plant?
Do you have a room closer to the bathroom?
When will the pool be built?
Will it be fixed during my stay here?

Do you think I should wear my purple-and-yellow-striped shirt with
     the green flowers or the pink one with the magenta tulips?
The truth—do I look like a tourist or a local?

Don't these three children approaching us look absolutely adora-
     ble?
Officer, do you ever catch any of those juvenile thieves?

◆

Yes, I'll pay, but don't you think seventy-eight dollars is a little steep
     for wooden salt and pepper shakers?
Are you really interested in hearing all about the birth of their God
     of Tree Barks?
Didn't I tell you to wear comfortable shoes?
Are warts considered a mark of beauty in your country?
Wouldn't you kill for a Big Mac?
Why can't they get their phones to work like ours?
Do you have to go to a specialist to have that bone put through your
     nose?
Why don't they have a sign: DON'T SLIP IN GOAT SHIT?
Does the forty dollars include the Cheez Whiz and the massage?

▲

Do you think the baboon barf will ruin the finish on the car?
Why do you think our President should do that to himself?
Why is everyone staring at us?
Are you having as difficult a time not gawking at those bare breasts
     as I am?
Should I put my arm around the statue?
Do you realize that if it weren't for us, you'd be saluting a German
     flag today?

Do you think they would feel around inside my cold cream for a
  bracelet?
You don't remember saying you would pack the converter?
Would you believe I thought I lost that bracelet we bought, not
  knowing it had fallen into my cold cream?

Why don't you just relax and enjoy yourself and diet when you get
  back home?
Who cares if I gain ten or fifteen pounds?

Do you wear the veil to bed?
How many times do I have to tell you that I don't want to ride your
  damn donkey?
How the hell should I have known that the only way up was by
  donkey?
Do we have to visit every church?
Did you have to take a whole roll of that eagle?
Why did you act like you understood every word he said?
Don't they sell deodorant in this country?
Can you see the face of Jesus in the rock?
Did Jesus ever wear a fedora?
Why did he get angry when I asked him if they ever change their
  chants?
How was I to know it was against their religion?
Do you really think this belt buckle was blessed by the Pope?
Why did he get so upset when I reminded him that Jesus and all
  his apostles were Jewish?
Are all these children yours?
You never heard of Bruce Springsteen, the Boss?

Did I or did I not say that no matter how slim the odds, I wanted us
  to get the cholera shots?
Are you going to let a lousy hair drier ruin our whole vacation?

Is it because of religion, superstition, or tradition that your women
    never shave?
Did he look deaf and blind to you?

◆

You really don't know people until you go on vacation with them,
    do you?
Did you hear the way he spoke to her?
Do you think we could get away from them for one afternoon?
No, why would I mind spending this lovely, sunny day going from
    one store to another?
Do you think the kids are okay?
Do you think my mother is okay?
Do you think the dog is okay?
Don't you miss anyone?

▲

Wouldn't you kill for a long, hot shower?
They call this toothpaste?
As a man, do you feel funny wearing a skirt?
Were you here during the bombings?
We call them "boobs"; what do you call them?

Is there anyone in the world you haven't bought a souvenir for?
Why should I ask when you're the one with the period?
Wasn't I the one who said I'd be just as happy hanging around the
    house for two weeks?

▲

★ ★ ★ Your Duty-Free Duty

Why do tourists buy duty-free alcoholic beverages? The obvious answer is, to save money. Let's look at what you actually save and what you have to do to get your savings.

Most duty-free shops are crowded with fellow bargain seekers, so the first thing you must do is fight the crowd. Next are forms you're going to have to fill out, but let's say you're a DFE—Duty-Free Expert—and can complete the questions sacrificing only ten minutes of your life. When you arrive home, you must carry the package off the plane, through the airport, and into your home. Okay, we'll say that you don't mind any of this. After all, look at what you saved.

Okay, let's look at what you saved. Let's say you bought four bottles. Assume that your local liquor store has no sales during the year where you can get a bargain on any of the bottles you bought. The full retail price is an average of $24 per bottle for a total of $96, and let's say that duty-free saves you a whopping 30 percent, for a total savings of $28.80.

Now, I want you to make believe you are standing in a foreign airport and I walk up to you and tell you that if you would get in line in a jam-packed store, fill out some forms for ten minutes, then carry a rather heavy package on and off a plane, into a cab or car, and into a house or apartment, then for doing all this, after a relaxing vacation, I'll give you $28.80. What would you say to me— and remember, there could be children within hearing range.

Let me toss in one more consideration. How often, when purchasing duty-free alcoholic beverages, have you bought a bottle of some never-before-experienced native drink? A bottle that, after you arrive home, is never opened or tasted once before it's sealed forever. If you haven't already given such a bottle away to friends for a holiday or special occasion, look at the price. I'll bet it's around $28.80.

Here's looking at ya, kid.

◆ ◆ ◆ **Too Long, Too Often**

You know you've been traveling too long or too often if, while you are away from home, you do any, or God help you, all, of the following:

- Start to miss your spouse.
- Watch Sermonette reruns.
- Begin to believe Jim Bakker.
- Think Tammy Faye Bakker wears too little makeup.
- Sing along with the TV sign-off national anthem.
- Definitely miss your spouse.
- Telephone someone you owe money.
- Look up your name in the local phone book for the second time.
- Call the person to tell them you have the same name.
- Invite Same Name to dinner.
- Begin thinking about having another child.
- Can't remember if you ever did have another child.
- Watch the local news with great interest.
- Visit the Greeting Card Museum.
- Call Housekeeping and ask if you could help out.
- Make your hotel bed and clean the bathroom a half hour before you check out.
- Count your fillings and give them names.
- Decide to learn how to write with the opposite hand.
- Try to name every left-handed ballplayer who ever lived.
- Count the number of Smiths and Joneses in the local phone book.
- Visit the Greeting Card Museum again.
- Make a list of every schoolteacher you had from kindergarten through high school.
- Add substitute teachers to the list.
- Start hanging out in the hotel lobby in hopes of finding a conversation.

- Start hanging out in the hotel lobby and talking to yourself.
- Talk to yourself, get into an argument with yourself, and lose.
- Get depressed over losing the argument.
- Read the hotel complimentary magazine cover to cover, word for word.
- Write the editor of the magazine a complimentary letter and ask for a subscription mailed to your house.
- Hand-wash your non-hand-washable suit or dress.
- Make a list of all American presidents.
- Make a list of all the vice-presidents.
- Make a list of all the things you would do were you the president.
- Decide to run for the presidency.
- Call the desk clerk "darling."
- Call your darling "desk clerk."
- Make a plan for the rest of your life, including meals.
- Try to remember the starting lineup of your sandlot baseball team.
- Think the housekeeper/maintenance person looks sexy.
- Pose for a picture in front of the cannon outside city hall.
- Send away for everything on the shoppers' channel.
- Decide to forgive everyone who has wronged you.
- Call all of them.
- Read the local classified section of the newspaper.
- Apply for jobs.
- Buy a cassette on learning Mandarin Chinese.
- Actually try to learn it.
- Decide to test it in the local Chinatown.
- Swear you will never eat eel testicles again.
- Read the obituaries.
- Attend the funerals of strangers.
- Steal the portrait of the hotel founder for your home.
- Sing your high school song.
- Clean out your wallet/pocketbook.
- Count the number of sheets on the toilet-paper roll to find out if the manufacturer lied.
- Write a letter of complaint to the manufacturer if it is short, and a complimentary letter if it is accurate.
- Read the Gideon Bible cover to cover.

- Write the author.
- Believe you are the author.
- Write your first fan letter.
- Remember the next day that Gabby Hayes is dead.
- Hand-write thank-you letters to every staff member in the hotel.
- Start a conversation with the cabdriver.
- Keep calling Correct Time, until you hear the hour change.
- Open a local checking account.
- Decide to change your name to "B. X. Rockmeyer."
- Sign up for volunteer work at the local hospital.
- Buy a hat for your boss.
- Buy a hat for your boss's spouse.
- Buy a hat for your boss's ex-spouse.
- Buy a hat for your ex-spouse.
- Go to a homeless shelter and give away hats.
- Accept the shelter's invitation to stay for dinner.
- Regret breaking your promise never to eat eel testicles again.
- Try to remember what was on TV at nine P.M. Wednesday nights during your last semester in high school.
- Decide Elvis is alive and living in Boonton, New Jersey.
- Make a list of every singer who has died in your lifetime.
- Start believing you had something to do with their deaths.
- Send copies of your room key to all your friends and relatives.
- Decide to change careers.
- Make a list of new careers.
- Decide to become a Viking.
- Rearrange the lobby furniture.
- Buy a barbecue and vacuum cleaner for your room.
- Vacuum your room, the hall, and the lobby.
- Go door-to-door trying to sell the vacuum.
- Start to like the paintings in your room.
- Call your answering machine and leave yourself a message.
- Call in the next day for your message.
- Rack your brain for the Spanish word for "onion."
- Examine your feet.
- Get angry all over again about high school prom night.
- Call your prom date and tell him or her off.
- Strain to remember the names of Donald Duck's nephews.

- Practice speaking like Donald Duck.
- Really like the haircut the hotel barber gave you.
- Write new lyrics for the song "My Way."
- After waving your hand to hail a cab and getting into one, you are still waving your hand to hail a cab.
- Never go out without exact change.
- Discover that as you continue traveling, your mind is narrowing instead of broadening.
- Know the skycaps by first names.
- Skycaps know you by your first name.
- Two hours after checking into a hotel, you are still wearing the airplane headset.
- Believe that no one in the world lives in a house.
- Open a Contac capsule and count the beads.
- Test how far you can throw a wet tea bag in the hall.
- Tie the DO NOT DISTURB sign around your neck.
- Put your overnight bag on your seat and then try to fit under the seat in front of you.
- Drive past a Fotomat booth and throw exact change inside.
- Start looking like your passport photo.
- Offer to Indian-leg-wrestle the bellhop for his tip.
- In shuffleboard, you cheat an old person.
- In a public bathroom stall, you try to get people to do the wave with you.
- Think of different ways to prepare Spam.
- Tell a strange woman with a floppy hat at the airport to get on the plane and not look back.
- Then, you look for a French cop with whom to walk away into the fog.
- Worry that everyone you know has forgotten you.
- Try to get a discussion group going on why most pandas are not fertile.
- Follow people selling sign-language cards to catch them talking.
- Take your suitcase to a garage to have the wheels rotated.
- With a Magic Marker, you make the greyhound dog on the side of your bus anatomically correct.
- Picket with the airline currently on strike.
- At a bus depot, you pair all the people who are talking to

themselves, so it looks as if they are carrying on normal conversations.

- Yank the turban off an Indian's head and see how many times you can towel-whip him before the police come.
- Try to organize races with everyone who has wheels on their suitcases.
- When the airport security alarm sounds as a passenger goes through, you yell, "Off with his head!"
- Organize an airport or bus depot glee club.
- Test how many times you can swivel on a restaurant stool before you throw up.
- Have been in so many cabs, you are fluent in nine languages.
- Can't believe you once dreamed of traveling.
- Answer to any first name.
- Believe seats aren't as comfortable as they used to be.
- Stop collecting receipts.
- Don't cheat on your expense account.
- Your expense account is off by over one million dollars and you don't care.
- Can't remember ever not standing in lines.
- Despise the Wright brothers.
- Don't mind waiting two days for room service.
- Try writing a country western song without mentioning a pickup truck, a drunk, an ex-mate, or a broken heart.
- Have the overwhelming desire to strangle as many street mimes as possible.
- Forget what your spouse looks like.
- Try to forget you have a spouse.
- Put on a puppet show in the lobby using your socks.
- Think the first day of the week is "Jorday."

▶ ▶ ▶ # Unaccustomed Customs

On every traveler's list of top-ten hates, customs has to be there. I'm sure it is also on the top-ten list of customs inspectors, as well. Customs inspections are not fun for the inspectors, either. My hat is off to all of them. It has to be, in order for them to look in the brim for contraband.

Customs inspection moves up the hate list in direct proportion to how long one has been traveling and according to how much irritation one has endured during the trip.

For twenty-eight sleepless hours, I had been sitting in airports listening to announcements about delayed and canceled flights, most of which were directly related to me, before I managed to get the last cramped seat in the smoking section of a rebuilt WWII Flying Fortress bomber that was being piloted by an escaped inmate of a Swedish insane asylum across a record-breaking turbulence over the Atlantic Ocean, none of which provided any relief for my lower back spasms and three-day losing battle with dysentery. As you might imagine, I was not in the best mood when we semi-crashed into the torrential-rain-soaked runway at JFK in the middle of the night.

Even after a night of comfortable, undisturbed sleep in a king-size bed, dressed meticulously, and in the best of health, for some reason, I still do not project honesty. Maybe it has something to do with growing up in the back streets and dark alleys of a bad big-city neighborhood. If, on the other hand, I am kept awake thirty-six hours, in pain and ill health, my aching body dressed in a smelly sweatshirt, crumpled jeans, and a pair of mud-encrusted high-top sneakers, I'll make Al Capone look like your friendly village blacksmith.

Even though I had been living these past four weeks on a rain-soaked island off the Swedish coast, producing a documentary on the life of filmmaker Ingmar Bergman, housed in a small fisherman's cabin void of such modern conveniences as washer and drier, I still managed to satisfy my omnipresent compulsion for neatness and cleanliness. Every article of clothing in my suitcase was spotlessly clean, neatly folded, and strategically placed. Had I lived in Pompeii when the volcano erupted, I would have been racing to beat the lava with a neatly packed overnight bag.

As always, the customs inspector took one look at me and asked me to open my bag. He proceeded to microscopically examine everything, to the extreme of squeezing my toothpaste out of the tube. Knowing that drug smuggling is a major problem, and luckily earning enough to purchase a new tube, I said nothing. I was also patient and understanding when he pulled the heel off one of my shoes. However, after he tore apart my bag and found nothing, I expected him to hand it back to me in the same condition as I handed it to him, but this was not the case. What was shoved toward me was a suitcase that couldn't even be closed because of the pile of what appeared to be a bag person's possessions.

"Next," called out the inspector.

"No next," called out this angry traveler.

"What?"

"Repack it!" I pointed to my suitcase.

"Move it," he demanded.

"Move this." I pointed to my crotch.

"You got a problem, pal?"

"You're my problem, pal," I hissed. "Get your supervisor over here, before I attach a handle to your ass and stuff my clothes down your throat!"

I told the people behind me to change lines, because I had a feeling this was going to be a long night.

When the supervisor and the two New York policemen arrived, I explained how I didn't mind my bag's being scrutinized, but that I wanted it returned to me in the exact condition I had handed it over. I announced that I wouldn't leave the airport until that was accomplished, and if this meant being arrested, I would surrender to New York's finest and talk to the press from my cell. The supervisor weighed his choices and voted in my favor. The line was officially closed and I supervised the repacking of my suitcase. I'd like to say that I'm the kind of person who does not take advantage of a situation, but I cannot say it, because I am.

"Excuse me, but I like my socks folded, not rolled, and placed in the suitcase with the darkest colors on the bottom and the lightest on the top. . . . No, my underwear gets folded with the fly facing up. . . . Sorry, the pants are put on the bottom so they stay pressed, so you'll have to start over. . . . Wow, you almost have all the toothpaste back in the tube. . . ."

Two hours later, I left the airport with both my suitcase and my value system intact. I was exhausted but elated. My father was right when he told me as a kid, "Go to the wall on a principle." This includes airport customs' walls.

▼ ▼ ▼ **If God Wanted Us to Travel . . .**

Other than to walk from one place to another very close by for something essential, to travel is one of mankind's most irrational, nonsensical, nonessential, idiosyncratic, and stupid pursuits, so I just have to believe that if God wanted us to travel . . .

—We would have built into our bodies luggage pouches like the kangaroo.
—He would not have allowed the DC-10 to be invented.
—Taxi drivers would have been given the tongue of the country in which they drive.
—He wouldn't have rested on the seventh day—he would have solved the traffic problem.
—Flight attendants wouldn't age so quickly.
—The Devil would not have been allowed to design airports.
—Children would be able to hold it in until they get there, no matter how long a trip.

—No one would have written the song "Ninety-nine Bottles of Beer on the Wall."
—Buses would smell better than old running shoes stuffed with rotten eggs.
—Trains wouldn't suddenly decide to go where they felt like going.
—Married people wouldn't be allowed to speak to one another while on vacation.
—Countries would be the same colors as they appear on maps. Same for states in the U.S.A.
—Children entering airplanes would turn into frogs.
—Babies on airplanes would have to ride in soundproof overhead compartments.
—Pets taken on public means of transportation could legally be cooked.
—Passengers sucked out of planes during flight would be entitled to frequent-traveler's mileage for their airborne time.
—Very fat people would have to be transported to their destinations on rotisseries.
—By pressing our belly buttons very hard, our asses would turn into parachutes and inflate.
—The same person who invented the indestructible black box would also have invented the airplane.
—The minute someone showed up somewhere, it would change to look as it does in its brochure.
—It would rain Coca-Cola in Mexico.
—There would be only one language in the world, and it would be "Igpay Atinlay."
—Everyone's passport picture would look like Matt Dillon and Michelle Pfeiffer.
—There would be only one golf course on only one island where all golfers would go.
—Fast food would be slow.
—Americans wearing Bermuda shorts with black ankle socks, loud voices, obnoxious personalities, and gargantuan asses would not be permitted to travel outside the USA.
—Until an airplane found a piece of your luggage they lost, you would have the right to hide one of their airplanes.
—The word *delayed* would not exist in any language.

—Anyone trying to force you out of your hotel room at the precise checkout time would turn into a warthog.

—Planes would fly no higher than ten to fifteen feet and would be made of soft, bouncy rubber.

—We would be frequent fliers from birth.

—Gas station rest rooms would be classified nuclear waste dumpsites.

—The man who designed the California freeway system would have been destined to spend his entire life on it.

—The people who invented vending machines in mass transportation facilities could be called at home to come over and kick a machine that kept your money.

—Airline mechanics would have to fly on every flight they check out.

—When your hotel room is bombarded by noise, the din would be transferred to the manager's bedroom in his home.

—Anyone unable to kick his foot against a telephone pole three times would not be allowed to become an airline ground mechanic or security inspector.

—Before anyone gives you a body search, they would have to give you a dozen long-stemmed roses and tell you they love you.

—At the end of a vacation, persons would automatically be entitled to an immediate vacation.

—After a customs guard searches your luggage, you could look through his wallet.

—Honeymooners would not be allowed to mingle with normal, realistic people.

—Anyone going on a "second honeymoon" would have to swear to the Almighty Himself that they really want to go.

—After you use hotel towels, they would be washed, dried, and mailed to your home.

—Every country would be as friendly as the locals of Saint Maarten, populated by people as physically beautiful as the Swedes, as emotional as Romans, and as romantic as Parisians, with food as delicious as that in St.-Tropez, be as mysteriously magnificent as Santorini, with a climate as wonderful as Bora-Bora's, and with a personality as explosively exciting as New York, as expansive as Australia, as nocturnal as Spain, as fascinating as Egypt, and as spiritual as Israel.

—Traveling would be so much fun and with so few hassles and irritations that no one would ever be able to write a humorous book about the subject. In other words, if God wanted us to travel, there couldn't be a book entitled *If God Wanted Us to Travel* . . .

♠ ♠ ♠ Epilogue

In 1986, I rented a thirteen-bedroom villa in St.-Tropez for one month. The main purpose was to have my elderly mother and father "hold court" over their three children, five grandchildren, other relatives, and my friends. Three months before we were to go, my eighty-six-year-old mother passed away in Singapore, halfway through her third world cruise. It was an extremely difficult time for all of us. Being together in the villa helped.

Understandably, hardest hit was my father. He and my mother had been together almost every day for sixty-five years. My father had always been a master of resilience and was trying his best to muster some. I dedicated myself to helping him. I tried to keep him as occupied as possible. Every day I took him and my son into St.-Tropez to sit in outdoor cafés, or for sight-seeing drives to neighboring towns. It was a very slow process. I wasn't sure it was working at all.

One of my father's loves for most of his life was driving a car. He taught all his children to drive, and none of us has ever had an accident. Whenever he could, he would take a ride or go on motor vacations with my mother. As long as he had a steering wheel in his hands, he was happy.

I tried coaxing him to drive several times, but he refused. One day, I just pulled the car onto the shoulder of the highway, walked around, opened his door, and shoved him over to the driver's seat. Three hours later, he parked the car in Monte Carlo. Over the remaining weeks, he would drive some of us to Monte Carlo, where he would hang out in the casino as we drove around sight-seeing.

215

We would pick him up at a time designated by him. I knew he was accepting life again.

After France, my father continued to travel, as he and my mother had done all their lives, regardless of how poor they were, and even after my mother lost her eyesight in the last years of her life. They loved to travel. Loved it!

In 1987, Lou Brenner, age ninety, went up the Mississippi aboard a paddleboat, took a train up and down California and over to Denver, made several trips to Las Vegas and to Atlantic City, spent many weeks hanging out with me in New York City, and sailed around the world for his fourth time.

In 1988, Lou Brenner, age ninety-one, passed away, just as he was completing his fifth world cruise, a little over two years after my mother died. Ironically, he died aboard the same cruise ship, in the same hospital, in the same bed as she.

Had my father lived, he would have spent one month during that summer in a villa I rented in Marbella, Spain, then would have joined me in Las Vegas for two weeks, followed by his already scheduled sixth trip around the world in September, and his seventh world cruise the following January.

The reason I have chosen this story for the epilogue is because I feel it best expresses how vital travel is for the human spirit, that you should never think you are too poor, too old, or too infirm to travel, and most importantly, that you should never give up, never stop living, not as long as there is a fraction of a breath remaining, as long as there is one more something of beauty you can see, one more experience you can capture, one more feeling you can grasp, one more moment of happiness, one more smile, one more laugh. All of this was demonstrated to me by my mother and father.

Do it! Go! It's your world!